Beyond Politics 2014:
And Undergraduate Review of Politics—Spring 2014

Beyond Politics:
An Undergraduate Review of Politics—Spring 2014

Beyond Politics

Department of Political Science
2014

First Printing: 2014

ISBN 978-1-312-10382-5

Department of Political Science]

Contents

Letter from the Editor

This year, Beyond Politics is moving in a new direction. We are embracing the digital age and moving our publication to an ebook format. As we continue establishing ourselves as an academic resource, we need to espouse the philosophies of our peer journals; that is, we need to aim beyond Notre Dame and publish so that the authors' work can truly become a part of the academic literature. It is my dream that this move will make Beyond Politics a fully sustainable endeavor that will become a major locus of the undergraduate practice of political science.

In working toward this goal, Beyond Politics has adopted a new philosophy of publication. Prior to this year, each issue focused on one subfield of political science, often to the detriment of political theory. As we establish ourselves among our respected peer journals, we need to showcase the best work done by our students, whether they are Comparativists, Americanists, Theorists, or students of International Relations. Thus, the articles published in this edition of Beyond Politics have been peer reviewed not according to their subfield, but by the merits of each individual paper. Beyond Politics is proud to say that these papers are representative of the work of Notre Dame undergraduate political science students and we believe each makes a creative and unique contribution to the field.

It has been a great opportunity to serve as the 2014 Editor-in-Chief of Beyond Politics, Notre Dame's Undergraduate Journal of Political Science. I am proud of what my peers at the University of Notre Dame have accomplished. As the Editorial Board worked through the reading process, I was humbled by the academic excellence of my peers. This Journal would not be possible without the dedicated Editorial Team that screened and edited papers for publication, Professor Carolina Arroyo whose administrative brilliance eased the transition to epublishing, Professor Dave Campbell whose insight and leadership guided the internal processes, and the Rooney Center for the Study of American Democracy who graciously provided funding.

Justin Sena '14
Editor-in-Chief

Soccer Wars
Christopher Newton

INTRODUCTION

In 1969, two member states of the Central American Common Market (CACM) went to war. El Salvador launched an undeclared assault on Honduras on July 14th. The conflict lasted 100 hours, ending with an Organization of American States orchestrated ceasefire on July 18th. The final tally of destruction included an estimated 2,000 battle deaths, 6,000 wounded, between 50,000 and 100,000 rendered homeless, and the near collapse of the CACM,[1] until then "one of the most successful movements for integration of regional economies".[2] No formal peace treaty was signed until 1980.[3] Two poor Central American nations, engaged in a successful economic integration scheme and unprepared for conflict, resorted to war despite serious economic and military limitations. Why?

This conflict is commonly known as the Soccer War. The actual causes of the war were not soccer matches, as numerous journalists and Westerners more generally believed. "Smart-aleck *gringo* journalists dubbed the conflict the "Soccer War" because its outbreak came on the heels of stadium riots during El Salvador-*vs-*Honduras World Cup playoffs".[4] Nationalism, overpopulation, and land monopolization have been used to explain the use of force by El Salvador. Each theory is supported by historical evidence. The objective of this paper is to determine which theory has the greatest explanatory power.

---

[1] Durham, William H. *Scarcity and Survival in Central America: Ecological Origins of the Soccer War*. Stanford, CA: Stanford UP, 1979. 1-2. Print.

[2] Betters, Elinor C., John Cobb, Jr., Johnathan A. Leonard, and Charles M. Townsend. Preface. *Area Handbook for El Salvador.* By Howard I. Blutstein. Washington: For Sale by the Supt. of Docs., U.S. Govt. Print. Off., 1971. V. Print.

[3] "GENERAL PEACE TREATY BETWEEN THE REPUBLICS OF EL SALVADOR AND HONDURAS." *United Nations Peacemaker*. United Nations, 17 Apr. 1980. Web. 13 Dec. 2013.

[4] Weinberg, Bill. *War on the Land: Ecology and Politics in Central America*. London: Zed, 1991. 29. Print.

The nationalism theory argues that crimes committed by Salvadorans and Hondurans against each other in 1969 led to strong nationalism in each country, leading El Salvador to attack Honduras to defend national honor and gain national prestige. This theory explains only part of the motivation of El Salvador to attack because it does not consider long-term resource scarcity in El Salvador. The overpopulation theory argues that high population growth led to resource scarcity in El Salvador and forced 300,000 Salvadorans to migrate to Honduras. El Salvador attacked Honduras in order to prevent the forced return of these migrants because El Salvador lacked the resources to feed them. This theory incorrectly uses overpopulation as the primary cause of resource scarcity in El Salvador. The land monopolization theory argues that high inequality in land ownership in El Salvador created artificial resource scarcity in that country. Artificial resource scarcity caused 300,000 Salvadorans to migrate to Honduras and El Salvador used force because domestic politics prevented land redistribution and the country did not have the resources to feed the migrants as a result.

The paper proceeds as follows: I first present the problem of the 300,000 Salvadoran migrants residing in Honduras at the time of the conflict and place it in a broader theoretical context. I then outline each theory and provide predictions for what would have been observed in the build-up to the Soccer War if they were the primary cause of war, with an emphasis on the question of the Salvadoran migrants. I then survey the evidence and find that the land monopolization theory explains the primary cause of the Soccer War and the nationalism and overpopulation theories provide secondary causes. I conclude with a discussion of generalizable findings derived from this analysis for inter-state war.

ON SALVADORAN MIGRANTS AND THE MATTER OF THEIR RETURN

By 1969, 300,000 Salvadoran migrants had come to reside in Honduras, representing roughly 10% of the population of El Salvador[5] and 12.5% of the population of Honduras.[6] It is important to question what about their return was intolerable for El Salvador, the aggressor

---

[5] Durham, 163.

[6] Durham, 2.

in the Soccer War. When the expulsions began in large numbers in June of 1969, El Salvador sealed its border with Honduras. When they continued, El Salvador launched a surprise attack on Honduras.[7] Even during the war, the question of the migrants was a prominent issue, if little understood outside of Central America. The New York Times noted that while there had been border skirmishes between the two countries for years, "a more important source of friction has been the migration over many years of perhaps 300,000 Salvadorans from their own incredibly crowded country to sparsely populated Honduras".[8] Each of the competing theories contends that the expulsion of Salvadoran migrants from Honduran territory played a critical role in the sparking of hostilities. This "issue is widely viewed as the key issue behind the Soccer War"[9] and is seen by many scholars as "the principal source of contention" between the two countries.[10]

Most international migration occurs from one developing nation to another. Such migration usually has its origins in political factors in the origin country. The larger the influx of migrants, the greater the threat the recipient country faces. While Myron Weiner identifies five separate threat types, the threat of social or economic burden is the most applicable to the Soccer War. This burden is greater when the migrants are poor and strain the recipient countries social services and economic resources.[11] Both scholars and the Salvadoran and Honduran governments report that the 300,000 migrants were largely from the lowest socio-economic class of El Salvador.[12] The tolerance for the perceived exporting of excess populations of burdensome poor people is also low in recipient countries.[13] This was true for Honduras in the 1960's. The country

---

[7] Durham, 2.

[8] "A Peace Task for the O.A.S." *The New York Times* [New York] 16 July 1969: 44. Print.

[9] Durham, 2.

[10] Bachmura, Frank T. "Toward Economic Reconciliation in Central America." *World Affairs* 133.4 (March, 1971): 283-92. Print.

[11] Weiner, Myron. "Security, Stability, and International Migration." *International Security* 17.3 (Winter 1992/93): 91-126. Print.

[12] Durham, 127.

[13] Weiner.

was ill equipped to handle the large influx of Salvadoran migrants; with a GDP 2/3 the size of El Salvador's by 1965.[14] Weiner offers three possible solutions to unwanted migrants: assist the origin country in resolving the issues that led to migration in the first place, put diplomatic pressure upon the origin country, or use force to either remove the migrants or to compel the origin country to curb migration.[15] Honduras chose to forcibly evict the Salvadoran migrants in an at times brutal fashion.[16]

Migration itself was not the primary cause of the Soccer War. It was El Salvador's refusal to countenance the return of the migrants that resulted in war. El Salvador rebuffed all attempts at diplomacy, instead launching a surprise attack. This intolerance for the return of the migrants is an intervening variable that all three leading theories agree upon. The primary cause of the Soccer War would explain what caused El Salvador's decision to initiate a war in response to the expulsion of the migrants. Each of the theories of the primary cause of war provide a variable that could explain the intolerance for the return of the Salvadoran migrants. In determining the primary cause it is then necessary to include predictions that relate to this intervening variable. See Figure 1 for the causal chain of the Soccer War.

Fig. 1 The Primary Cause of the Soccer War: What Caused Intolerance for the Return of the Migrants?

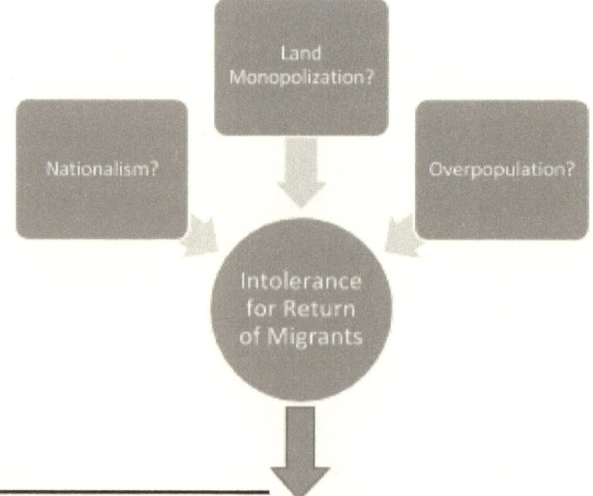

[14] Weeks, John. *The Economies of Central America*. New York: Holmes & Meier, 1985. 48. Print.

[15] Weiner.

[16] Bachmura.

```
┌─────────────────┐
│  Decision to Go │
│     to War      │
└─────────────────┘
```

THEORIES AND PREDICTIONS OF THE PRIMARY CAUSE OF THE SOCCER WAR

Nationalism has often been cited as a cause of inter-state war. I use a modified form of a definition of nationalism provided by Rupert Emerson and Richard Cottam. They define it as "a belief on the part of a large group of people that they comprise a community, a nation, which is entitled to independent statehood, and a willingness of this group to grant their community a primary and terminal loyalty".[17] To this definition I add that this perceived community by the individuals within the group is an integral component of each individual's identity. Thus in threatening or offending the community, the individual is also threatened or offended.

Stephen Van Evera provides a series of hypotheses that predict nationalism causing war under a variety of circumstances. He offers two hypotheses regarding political/environmental factors and perceptual factors that are relevant to the Soccer War. The political/environmental factors hypothesis states that "The greater the past crimes committed by nationalities toward one another, the greater the risk of war".[18] Corollaries of this hypothesis include increased risk of war as a result of remembrance of crimes, enduring group responsibility, and a lack of repentance by the perpetrator. The perceptual hypothesis argues that "The more divergent are the beliefs of nationalities about their mutual histories and their current conduct and character, the greater the risk of war".[19] Corollaries of this hypothesis include increased risk of war as a result of large demands placed upon the citizenry by the government, poor economic

---

[17] Evera, Stephen Van. "Hypothesis on Nationalism and War." *The MIT Press* 18.4 (Spring, 1994): 5-39. Print.

[18] Van Evera, 1994.

[19] Van Evera, 1994

conditions, and weak independent, evaluative institutions. Table 1 reproduces Van Evera's hypotheses in full.

Table 1   Stephen Van Evera's Nationalism Hypotheses

Political/Environmental Factors	Perceptual Factors
1. The greater the past crimes committed by nationalities toward one another, the greater the risk of war.	2. The more divergent are the beliefs of nationalities about their mutual histories and their current conduct and character, the greater the risk of war
a) The better these crimes are remembered by the victims, the greater the risk of war.	a) The more the state must demand of its citizens, the greater its propensity to purvey nationalist beliefs, hence the greater the risk of war.
b) The more responsibility for past crimes can be attached to groups still on the scene, the greater the risk of war.	b) If economic conditions deteriorate, publics become more receptive to scapegoat myths, hence such myths are more widely believed, hence war is more likely.
c) The less contrition and repentance shown by the guilty groups, the greater the risk of war.	c) If independent, evaluative institutions are weak or incompetent, myths will more often prevail, hence war is more likely.

In the case of the Soccer War, nationalism was pervasive following riots after the first of two World Cup qualifying matches in June and early July of 1969, weeks before the outbreak of the war. If this theory was a primary cause of war, the occurrence of crimes against individuals identifying themselves as of Salvadoran nationality by individuals identifying themselves as of Honduran nationality, and vice versa, would be observed. There would be collective blame assigned by one or both sides, extensive media coverage of alleged offenses, and discussion among political leaders El Salvador of national honor and prestige motivating military decisions. There would be a lack of repentance by each side and a lack of dissenting opinions in public discussions, especially by media. Strong demands placed upon the citizenry and deteriorating economic conditions in El Salvador would also increase nationalism and the likelihood of war. In terms of the migrant question, crimes would have been committed or perceived to have been committed against the 300,000 migrants in Honduras by Hondurans, their expulsion would have been seen as illegal by El Salvador, Hondurans would see the presence of the migrants as a crime and offensive to Honduras, and neither side would have repented for actions related to migrants.

The second theory for the causes of the Soccer War is that of overpopulation. This theory stems from a Neo-Malthusian school of thought regarding the causes of war. T. R. Malthus's basic argument was that "the power of population to grow was "indefinitely greater" than the power of the earth to produce subsistence".[20] Neo-Malthusians view population growth as the source of many of mankind's problems and "the most pressing political-economic problem of our time".[21] As it relates to war, the argument is that in modern society, Malthus' positive checks on population, such as disease and famine, have largely been mitigated. Population growth, particularly in developing countries, is rapid. This population growth places pressure on economic and social structures and reduces the availability of national resources. Nations must seek to accommodate their burgeoning populations and "Obviously, the human mind will not revert to pestilence or famine". "Resort to arms is the only positive check left to meet and adjust economic pressure according to Neo-Malthusian theory" and "war, then, is not merely a possibility of economic pressure, but is in the nature of an economic certainty".[22]

---

[20] Winch, Donald. *Malthus: A Very Short Introduction.* Oxford: Oxford UP, 2013. 20. Print.

[21] Ehrlich, Paul R., and Anne H. Ehrlich. *Population Resources Environment: Issues in Human Ecology.* San Francisco, CA.: W.H. Freeman, 1970. 311. Print.

In examining this theory, attention must be focused on the aggressor in the Soccer War, El Salvador. The logic of Neo-Malthusianism dictates that a country facing significant overpopulation would act to rectify the problem and alleviate the pressures of excess population through war. High population growth and population density were present in El Salvador in the in the 1960's. If it was the primary cause of war, high population growth, high population density, insufficient domestic food production, low socio-economic indicators, high landlessness, and discussions among government leaders of overpopulation as a significant national issue and as a motivation for military action would be observed in El Salvador. The conclusion that El Salvador could not support its population with the national resources it possessed at the time of war must be strongly supported. As this relates to the migrants, overpopulation would have been a primary motivation for the Salvadorans leaving El Salvador. The return of the migrants would be seen as a threat to El Salvador by its leaders on the grounds that they could not be supported and represented an unacceptable strain on El Salvador's resources.

The final theory is that of land monopolization. This borrows from theories of war involving environmental decline. This school of thought holds that changes in the environment of a given territory may lead to adverse social effects such as reduced agricultural output, economic decline, population displacement, and the disruption of regular and legitimized social practices. These effects in turn cause social tension, which may lead to intra or inter-state conflict. The environmental change that prompts such social tension may be naturally occurring or anthropomorphic.[23] The key mechanism that translates environmental change into conflict is the inherent increase in social tension from declining resource availability. The land monopolization theory focuses on anthropomorphic environmental decline. Mismanagement of resources led to their artificial scarcity and led to war.

"Agriculture is the main source of income, jobs, and government revenue in Central America".[24] When arable land is

[22] James, Edwin W. "The Malthusian Doctrine and War." *The Scientific Monthly* 2.3 (March, 1916): 260-71. Print.

[23] Homer-Dixon, Thomas F. "On the Threshold: Environmental Changes as Causes of Acute Conflict." *International Security* 16.2 (Fall 1991): 76-116. Print.

misused, the consequences are significant. It has led many scholars to the following conclusion: "What is at the root of Central America's war and crisis? The answer can be summed up in a single word: land".[25] John Weeks states that "The ownership and distribution of land is the primary political issue in Guatemala, El Salvador, and Honduras...".[26] Extreme land inequality in El Salvador led to a situation in which resources became scarce, social tensions rose dramatically, and war became highly likely.

If this theory of land monopolization leading to artificial environmental decline is the primary cause of the Soccer War, massive inequality in land ownership, high rates of landlessness, the domination of non-subsistence agriculture, an artificial decline in food production, social unrest related to landlessness, and the political dominance of wealthy landowners would be observed in El Salvador. On the matter of the migrants, the return of the migrants would be intolerable for El Salvador due to an artificial inability to accommodate them. Government leaders would highlight the inability of the nation to handle the influx, the threat the migrants' return posed to the country, the artificial nature of the land crisis in their discussions, and domestic political constraints related to their ability to alleviate the land crisis. The threat to El Salvador would be viewed as significant enough to warrant military action.

EVIDENCE AND THE PRIMARY CAUSE OF THE SOCCER WAR

Even strong opponents of the Neo-Malthusian theory admit that "At first glance, El Salvador does appear to provide an excellent argument for the Malthusian model of resource scarcity".[27] El Salvador has a land area of approximately 8,000 square miles and is roughly 1/6th the size of Honduras, which has a land area of approximately 43,000 square miles. In 1969, El Salvador had a population of 3.3 million over double the population of 1.5 million in

---

[24] Barry, Tom. *Roots of Rebellion: Land & Hunger in Central America.* Boston: South End, 1987. 4. Print.

[25] Weinberg, 5.

[26] Weeks, 34.

[27] Durham, 21.

Honduras. From 1930 to 1961, the population of El Salvador almost doubled from 1.4 million to 2.5 million. Throughout the 1960's, the average annual growth rate of the population was 3.5%.[28] El Salvador at the time of the Soccer War was the most densely populated country in the Western Hemisphere and had a population density in 1968 of 403 people per square mile[29], greater than that of India at the time.[30] In 1969, the population density of arable land alone was 782 people per square mile, compared to only 155 in Honduras.[31]

To feed this rapidly expanding population with limited arable land, food imports into El Salvador doubled between 1952 and 1962.[32] Both El Salvador and Honduras were identified by the United Nations in the late 1960's as "food priority countries" due to low average incomes, projected shortfalls in cereals production, and massive nutritional deficits.[33] It seemed logical to many that El Salvador was outstripping its available resources through rapid population growth and the Soccer War had highlighted the country's "basic problem of overpopulation.[34] Paul Ehrlich argues that the 300,000 Salvadorans migrated "because of the population pressure" in El Salvador.[35]

In a frequently cited 1976 Environmental Fund statement, leading population experts asserted that "World food production cannot keep pace with the galloping growth of population...Population growth has pushed the peoples of Africa, Asia, and Latin America onto lands which are only marginally suitable for agriculture".[36] Such sentiments seemed to reflect public opinion at the time as well. A letter to the editor published in the New York Times, following the Soccer War, asked "How many more conflicts will result from the population crush?".[37] The

---

[28] Betters et al, 50.

[29] Betters et al, 50.

[30] Durham, 6.

[31] Ehrlich, 311.

[32] Browning, David. *El Salvador: Landscape and Society.* Oxford: Clarendon, 1971. 301. Print.

[33] Wortman, Sterling. "Food and Agriculture." *Scientific American* 235.3 (1976): 31-39. Print.

[34] Browning, 22.

[35] Ehrlich, 311.

[36] Weinberg, 153.

[37] ""Soccer War" Causes." Editorial. *New York Times* [New York] 5 Aug.

overpopulation theory maintains that El Salvador could not accommodate the return of the migrants because the same food and land shortages that had prompted their exit were still occurring. After this first glance, however, overpopulation theory loses explanatory power.

The overpopulation theory only serves as a secondary cause of the Soccer War. Overpopulation exacerbated the adverse social effects of land monopolization, but did not instigate war. Given that "the Central American countries are not predominantly wage-labor societies"[38] and the aforementioned predominance of agriculture and land use, it is necessary to examine in detail the geography of El Salvador and Honduras and the land policies of each country.

There are three main bioregions in Central America. They consist of the Pacific Coastal Plain, the Central Highlands, and the Caribbean Zone. These zones provide ideal conditions for growing cotton, coffee, and bananas, respectively. The Pacific Coastal Plain is a narrow strip of land that contains some of the most fertile soil on the planet. This plain, along with portions of the Central Highlands, are fertilized by deposits of volcanic ash from the volcanoes present in the central portion of Central America. Most Central American nations have their highest population densities along their Pacific coast.[39] See Figure 2 for a map of volcano locations in Central America. El Salvador benefits greatly from these volcanoes, possessing large portions of Pacific Coastal Plain and fertile Central Highlands land. Thomas Anderson has quipped that "There seems to be a rule in El Salvador that every major city must have its own volcano".[40] El Salvador thus had perfect land conditions for large-scale, commercial agriculture for export or the means to sustain a large population, but not both simultaneously.[41]

Fig. 2   Volcanoes of Central America

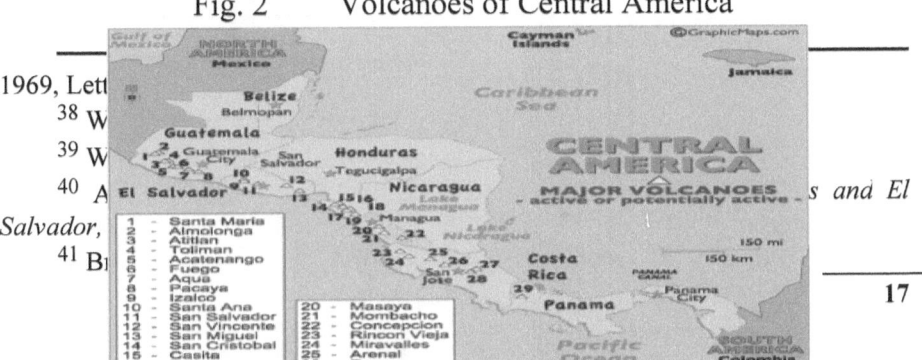

1969, Lett
38 W
39 W
40 A
Salvador,
41 B

s and El

Honduras has been constrained agriculturally. It lacks the volcanic ash-fertilized regions of El Salvador and is dominated by the Central Highlands and Caribbean Zone, with limited Pacific Coastal Plain. These zones are dominated by tropical rainforest. Although these zones see rainfall year-round, their soil is of poor quality. These rainforests are incapable of sustaining most forms of long-term agriculture. "In fact, they are really not appropriate for much of anything other than supporting rainforest...90 percent of the nutrients in the rainforest are in the vegetation itself".[42] The mountains of the Central Highlands also cover the majority of the land in Honduras, rendering it unsuitable for agriculture. 60.8% of the land in Honduras has a slope greater than 40%, making it unusable. See Figure 3 for an elevation map of Central America. Honduras has always had very low population densities in its interior, particularly along its border with El Salvador. As a result of its poorer soil quality, Honduras also has lower agricultural yields than El Salvador. It sees roughly half the per hectare yield of maize of El Salvador.[43]

Fig. 3 Elevation in Central America[44]

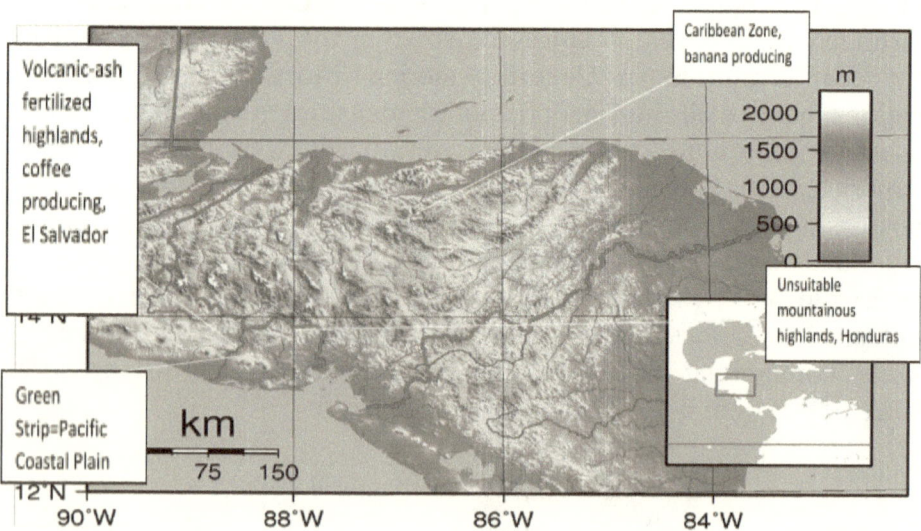

---

[42] Weinberg, 22.

[43] Durham, 107-109.

[44] "Geography of Honduras." *Wikipedia.* Wikimedia Foundation, 12 Dec. 2013. Web. 14 Dec. 2013.

Historically, Central America has maintained a dense, large population relative to the rest of the world. Prior to the arrival of Europeans in 1492, the region was the mostly densely populated region in the world. It has even been argued that before the time of Columbus' first voyage, more people lived in the Americas overall than in Europe.[45] These serve as major historical counterarguments to the overpopulation theory. It is clear that the way the land is used has changed, making current populations unsustainable. It was the arrival of the Spanish colonizers in Central America that drastically altered the agricultural techniques used in the region and devastated the local population, with an estimated 95% of the indigenous population eliminated over the first 130 years, largely due to disease.[46]

The privately controlled, large scale agriculture of the Spanish rapidly depleted the nutrients of the soil and severely damaged the local ecology in the lands they controlled. Their system replaced the communal, sustainable subsistence system of the indigenous population and promoted the extreme concentration of land ownership still seen today.[47] The oligarchic system of land control of the Spanish endured for centuries in Central America, even after independence in the early 1800's. "Spain laid the foundations for a Central American oligarchy through a land grants system, in which a small number of Spanish families were given control over the region's main resource-land".[48] Despite numerous attempts at land reform since independence, by the time of the Soccer War no Central American nation had succeeded in redistributing land. It is helpful here to quote Tom Barry at length, written 18 years after the Soccer War:

"The main elements of Central America's agroexport system-large landholdings, oligarchic control, and a repressed labor force-persist, despite the broadening of the economy and modernization of agricultural production. The changes in the economy and society have occurred without substantially altering old patterns of land and labor.

[45] Mann, Charles C. *1491: New Revelations of the Americas before Columbus.* New York: Knopf, 2005. 94. Print.

[46] Mann, 92.

[47] Weinberg, 7-9.

[48] Barry, 44.

In fact, the oligarchy's hold on the region's land, labor, and politics has tightened with the development of each new agroexport".[49]

The economies of Central America have depended almost entirely on agroexport, the export of cash crops, for economic growth and foreign currency since independence. Through the development of agroexport, land concentration increased. Agroexport crops provide only seasonal labor and do not sustain peasants year-round. El Salvador formally abolished communal land rights in 1881, allowing for a full private takeover of the nation's arable land.[50] Coffee plantations soon dominated the fertile highlands, displacing subsistence farmers to other regions. From 1915 to 1928, coffee exports tripled from $7.372 million to $22.741 million. At the same time, food production began its decline. Following the rise in agroexport and the decline in food production was a population recovering from colonization.

By 1890, the population of El Salvador had risen to pre-Columbian levels. [51] Tensions over land were on the rise between the landed elite and the increasingly displaced masses. When the global economy crashed in 1929, 350 upper-class Salvadoran families took the opportunity to organize and buy-out large numbers of small landowners, further concentrating land ownership. A reformist government came to power in 1931 with the idea of redistributing land and easing the mounting social tensions in the agrarian nation. It was toppled in a coup backed by the wealthy landowners in 1932. In response, the disenfranchised peasant population revolted.[52] Roughly 1% of the population of El Salvador perished in what is now referred to as La Matanza, the Killing.[53] The subdual of this revolt suppressed the anger and frustration of the peasant population in the short-term. Agroexport continued to expand and displace more Salvadoran peasants. In the 1930's a cotton boom began in El Salvador. Cotton gradually took over the fertile Pacific Coastal Plain, the breadbasket

---

[49] Barry, 46.

[50] Anderson, 16-17.

[51] Anderson, 13-14.

[52] Anderson, 19-20.

[53] Durham, 43-44.

of Central America. Between 1935 and 1965, cotton acreage increased from 1,144 hectares to 110,792 hectares.[54]

As coffee came to dominate to dominate the highlands and cotton the lowlands in El Salvador, poor Hondurans fared no better. United Fruit Company began in the early 1900's to purchase thousands of hectares of Honduras' arable land in the Caribbean Zone, its most fertile region. Through the violent intimidation and bribery of Honduran politicians, including the overthrow of the incumbent regime when the company first arrived in 1910, United Fruit came became a powerful and successful company.[55] In 1959, *Fortune* noted of United Fruit that "in Guatemala, Costa Rica, and *Honduras*, it is still the largest single private landowner, largest single business, and largest corporate employer" (emphasis added).[56] United Fruit came to control vast amounts of land in plantations and railroads. It even provided basic services for its employees and their families that far surpassed those provided by the government.[57]

United Fruit came to own over 300,000 acres by the early fifties and, "in relation to the economy of Honduras, it was four times as important as was General Motors to the economy of the United States…Altogether, the banana industry, because of its influence in government land policy, its inducements for Salvadoran labor, and its economic control of the government, would play a large part in creating the conditions which to led war in 1969".[58] Land concentration, primarily among the domestic landed elite in El Salvador and foreign fruit companies in Honduras, set the two nations on track for a major crisis of land.

Before proceeding, it is necessary to note an axiom of the peasant class of Central America. The campesinos of Central America, the peasant class, will relocate to uncultivated land when displaced. They will find available land, be it claimed by the wealthy already or not, and cultivate for their own subsistence. This was

---

[54] Anderson, 29.

[55] McCann, Thomas P., and Henry Scammell. *An American Company: The Tragedy of United Fruit*. New York: Crown, 1976. 17-19. Print.

[56] McCann, 61.

[57] Anderson, 47-49

[58] Anderson.

observed in both Honduran and Salvadoran peasant populations at the time of the Soccer War.[59] This process was made all the more feasible due to the low rates of cultivation by the wealthiest landowners, particularly in Honduras. In areas of low soil quality, it is necessary to allow land to lie fallow for 2-3 years. As such, farms with 50 or more hectares only had approximately 7% of their land under cultivation at a given time in Honduras.[60] In El Salvador, farms larger than 50 hectares only cultivated 35% of their available land at a given time.[61] In struggling for survival, peasants have no qualms about infringing upon the uncultivated lands of the wealthy. David Browning conveys, as shown in Table 2, the dichotomy of exploitive agroexport cultivation by the few and small-scale subsistence farming by the many:

"Each year the acres of coffee, sugar, cotton, and henequen are viewed by the *hacendado* as his personal possessions and the reward for his ownership, organization and the use of the land. The *campesino*, whether he be cash tenant, seasonally employed migrant, *aparcero*, *colono*, or squatter, regards the land about him as his ally in the daily struggle of gaining his living".[62]

Table 2   Dichotomy of Competing Land Systems in Central America, 19th-20th Centuries

Agroexport Agriculture	Subsistence Agriculture
Primarily for Export	Primarily for Domestic, Local Consumption
Large-scale, Land Intensive	Small-scale, Small Amounts of Land
Dominated by Wealthy Elite, Significant Minority	Dominated by Poor Masses, Significant Majority
Land Use for Profit	Land Use for Survival
Private Ownership	Communal Ownership

After World War II, Central American agricultural exports increased and the agroexport sector grew at a rate never before seen.

---

[59] Browning, 297-300.

[60] Durham, 127.

[61] Durham, 51.

[62] Browning, 293.

With the competition from Pacific nations removed following the war, Central America had room for expansion.[63] Across Central America, from 1950 to 1979, cotton production increased 10-fold and coffee production doubled while land devoted to food production dropped between 30% and 60% as it gave way to export crops.[64] Weeks observed that "In few areas of the world is such a large proportion of agricultural land devoted to products which the local population does not consume or consumes only to a limited degree".[65] The expansion of agroexport in the 1950's and 1960's "intensified grievances and conflicts in the countryside" across Central America, with El Salvador a notable case in its failure to reform land policy in response.[66]

Post-World War II, as a result of increases in agroexport, land concentration reached unprecedented levels in both El Salvador and Honduras. In Honduras, 8.8% of the population controlled 63.3% of the land by 1969. In El Salvador, by 1960 0.01% of the population controlled 16% of the land.[67] By 1961, 2% of the Salvadoran population owned 60% of the land.[68]The proportion of the population listed as landless peasants in El Salvador increased from 11% to 40% from 1961 to 1975.[69] This process of increasing agroexport production led to mass landlessness and subsequent pauperization of large segments of Salvadoran and Honduran society. It also led to an artificial food crisis as food-producing peasants were displaced by cash crops for export. Despite the fertility of El Salvador, by the time of war malnutrition affected 80% of children under 5.[70]

This process of displacement by agroexport forced the peasant populations of both countries into the interior of Central America in search of land to produce food for survival. As the best arable land

---

[63] Weeks, 26.

[64] Barry, 40-43.

[65] Weeks, 102.

[66] Kay, Cristóbal. "Reflections on Rural Violence in Latin America." *Third World Quarterly*22.5 (2001): 741-75. Print.

[67] Anderson, 17.

[68] Anderson, 31-32.

[69] Weinberg, 152.

[70] Durham, 7.

was taken for cash crops, peasants turned to the low-soil quality of the interior rainforests in Honduras. In El Salvador, due to the predominance of high quality soil, peasants had nowhere to turn for new land. Wherever the soil could support cash crops, the landed elite had claimed it. The low-soil quality of rainforests has made them "political safety valves" for many Central American nations, new "agricultural frontiers" undesired by agroexport to which displaced peasants may turn to sustain themselves.[71] Thus Salvadorans were forced to seek land in rainforest-covered Honduras, unable to find low-quality land in their own country.

El Salvador faced a land crisis before Honduras and the first waves of migrants were able to occupy Honduran land with no issue. As land became scarce in Honduras, Honduran peasants moved into the less fertile regions in the previously low-population density highlands. The displaced masses of the two countries, upon encountering one another, stayed true to the axiom of the Central American peasant. Both nationalities of peasants began squatting on the uncultivated land of wealthy Honduran landowners.

By 1969, Salvadoran migrants had come to comprise 20% of active agriculturalists in Honduras.[72] United Fruit and wealthy Honduran landowners were clamoring for the eviction of Salvadoran migrants and the removal of all peasants from their lands. The Honduran government passed a law allowing for the eviction of migrants in 1963, not implemented until 1969.[73] Before 1969, peasants reported bearing no ill will towards peasants of the other nationality, acknowledging the universal need to find land.[74] Unlike in El Salvador throughout the 1960's, there was no more land to displace peasants to in Honduras, except back into land-scarce El Salvador. The situation escalated over the course of the 1960's and outpaced the traditional pace of reform in the two countries.[75]. The number of Salvadoran migrants in the region increased from an estimated 38,002 in 1961 to an estimated 300,000 by 1969. The stage was set for the

---

[71] Barry, 110-111.

[72] Durham, 125.

[73] Durham, 8.

[74] Durham, 160.

[75] Mundigo, Axel I. *Elites, Economic Development, and Population in Honduras.* Diss. Cornell University, 1972. 83. Print.

Soccer War. See Figure 4 for the migration patterns of Salvadoran and Honduran peasants.

Fig. 4 The Migration of Peasants in Honduras and El Salvador

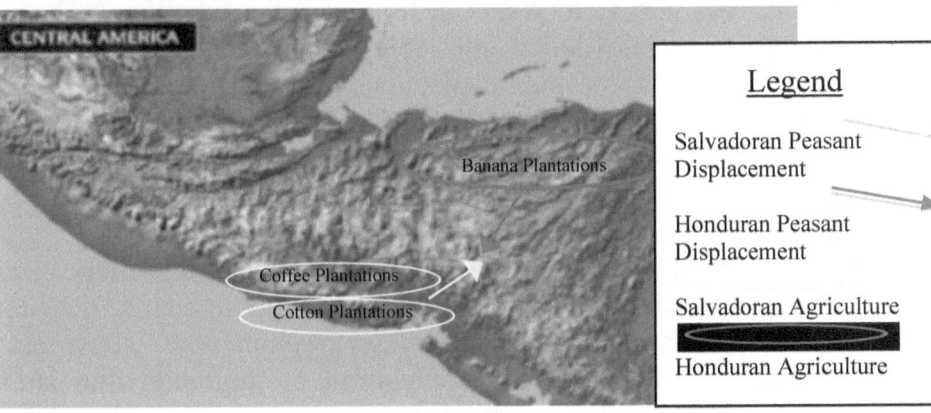

76

Process-tracing indicates that this is the narrative that policy-makers in El Salvador discussed when deciding whether or not to initiate hostilities. In 1972, in examining the failure of international development programs since World War II in Central America, Gary Wynia found that government leaders, including the Presidents of several countries including El Salvador and Honduras, explicitly stated their fear of the wealthy landowners. These political leaders "very carefully acknowledged the policy claims of their societies' most powerful groups, particularly those associated with export agriculture".[77] He also found that, since 1960, Salvadoran presidents' responses to the grievances of the poor have "been limited by the...recurrent economic elite opposition to resource expanding reform measures".[78] To threaten these interest groups was to threaten

---

[76] "Remote Sensing Tutorial Page 6-11." *Remote Sensing Tutorial Page 6-11*. RST, n.d. Web. 13 Dec. 2013.

[77] Wynia, Gary W. *Politics and Planners; Economic Development Policy in Central America*. [Madison]: University of Wisconsin, 1972. 192. Print.

[78] Wynia, 196.

the very survival of their governments. These confessions form the long-term basis of El Salvador's intolerance for the return of the migrants. The domestic land and political situation could not tolerate their return and the government faced possible collapse if they were allowed to do so.

After the war, then President of El Salvador Fidel Sanchez Hernandez, in a victory speech following the cessation of hostilities, "as if to acknowledge the role of land concentration in the conflict...called for public discussion of land reform and laid the groundwork for the First National Congress of Agrarian Reform".[79] It should also be noted that large landowners opposed this endeavor and within three months "the Legislative Assembly bowed to the pressure, and so stiffly amended the project as to annul it".[80]

On the Honduran side, there were strong beliefs as to the motivations of El Salvador. A well-known politician at the time and former cabinet member, on condition of anonymity, stated that "The war resulted from the lack of control of migration into Honduras which has brought about many problems for us and whose gestation dates to many years ago...[Expulsion] provoked anger among certain Salvadorean sectors who had taken it for granted that Honduras was the valve of escape for their excess population".[81] A lower-ranking government official at the time of war, on condition of anonymity, asserted that "In El Salvador, all the land is in the hands of a few large latifundists but the territory has an area of 30,000 square kilometers (currently 21,000 sq. km.)...The real problem in El Salvador is land distribution. Here, on the other hand, we have immense unexploited wealth. Therefore they kept sending people to our country-the worst, not the best type".[82]

In answering the question of why migrants were moving from a more developed country to a less developed country, another Honduran politician, on condition of anonymity, claimed "Their agrarian problems result from concentration of land in the hands of a few wealthy families while the majority of the peasants must face sub-human living conditions".[83] This assessment of the living

---

[79] Durham, 165-166.

[80] Durham, 166-167.

[81] Mundigo, 82.

[82] Durham, 89.

conditions in El Salvador was not unique to Honduran politicians, with the OAS Human Rights Commission agreeing. After investigating accusations of crimes against Salvadoran migrants in Honduras in 1969, one member of the Commission concluded that "The violation of human rights is that one country can't support 300,000 of its people...that they have to leave, not to seek a life of luxury, no, but to try for a limited life in another poor country little better prepared to support them".[84]

Closer to the actual initiation of war, Salvadoran leaders discussed the possibility of war with Honduras in advance. In June of 1968, amidst repeated border clashes, former Salvadoran President Osmin Aguirre y Salinas issued the following statement: "We should respond as strongly as did Israel to its "half-brother" Arabs in June 1967. If you do this, Col. Sanchez Hernandez and 75% of the patriotic Salvadorenos will be with you to the end and beyond".[85] Sources close to the Salvadoran army also revealed that military planning had begun on June 1st, in anticipation of hostilities in the coming months.[86] It must be remembered that the eviction of Salvadoran migrants from Honduras began in the beginning of June, 1969. The beginning of military planning in El Salvador directly coincided with the onset of evictions. This is evidence against the nationalism theory, as the first qualifying match, and the beginning of the tension between the Salvadoran and Honduran publics, was June 8th, a full week later.[87] It is clear that the surprise attack was pre-meditated in response to the large-scale evictions and not a knee-jerk reaction to nationalistic outrage. While nationalism hastened the process of military escalation, it did not begin it.

In an interview with then President Hernandez, Anderson reports that the President believed "the situation with the refugees had become intolerable and that El Salvador therefore made a quick decision to attack to put pressure on Honduras to reform its anti-

---

[83] Durham, 86.

[84] Diuguid, Lewis H. ""Soccer War" Still Smolders." *The Washington Post* [Washington, D.C.] 12 July 1969: A33. Print.

[85] Anderson, 111.

[86] Anderson, 110.

[87] Anderson, 110.

Salvadoran policy".[88] He also noted "the great pressure he was under from public opinion and his own military, declaring that if had not invaded on the fourteenth, there would have been a coup in twenty-four hours".[89] While this may at first appear to be an unverifiable excuse, it must be noted that coups were common practice in Central America at the time, with El Salvador's most recent coup having occurred 9 years prior. See Table 3 for a tabulation of successful coups in Central America by country.

Table 3   Successful Coups Since Independence by Country in Central America Up to 1969

Guatemala	El Salvador	Honduras	Nicaragua	Costa Rica	Panama
3	3	3	2	3	1

[90](Belize did not gain independence until 1981)[91]

This explicit mention of public pressure does lend credence to the nationalism theory and requires an examination of the domestic atmosphere in El Salvador in the weeks leading up to war. While long-term evidence is lacking for this theory, short-term evidence is present. Nationalist sentiment was pervasive following the first two of three qualifying matches for the 1970 World Cup between El Salvador and Honduras. The first match was played in Honduras on Sunday, June 8th. The Salvadoran team was "the target of psychological warfare waged by the Honduran fans" the night before the game, ensuring they slept little.[92] Honduras won the match the following day, 1-0.

Amelia Bolanios, an 18 year-old Salvadoran girl, reacted to the loss by committing suicide immediately. The following day a major Salvadoran newspaper reported "The young girl could not bear to see her fatherland brought to its knees".[93] The rest of the country

[88] Anderson, 111.

[89] Anderson, 111.

[90] Salmon, Felix. "Dates of Successful Latin American Coups." *Rueters*. Rueters, 29 June 2006. Web. 14 Dec. 2013; Durham; Anderson.

[91] "Central Intelligence Agency." *The World Factbook*. Central Intelligence Agency, n.d. Web. 12 Dec. 2013.

[92] Kapuściński, Ryszard. *The Soccer War*. New York: Knopf, 1991. 157. Print.

[93] Kapuściński, 158.

could not accept the outcome either, as "the whole capital took part in the televised funeral of Amelia Bolanios. An army honour guard marched with a flag at the head of the procession. The president of the republic and his ministers walked behind the flag-draped coffin."[94] The participation by the highest levels of the Salvadoran government in this public, soccer-related funeral indicate the intense emotions of the public at the time.

The second qualifying match was played in the capital of El Salvador, San Salvador. Enraged Salvadorans kept the Honduran national team awake the entire night before the second match on June 15th. El Salvador won handily 3-0 the next day. The Honduran team required an army escort and transportation by armored car to and from the stadium. During pregame ceremonies, the Honduran flag was burned and the Salvadorans instead "ran a dirty, tattered dishrag up the flag pole".[95] In the aftermath, two Honduran fans were killed and 150 Honduran fans' cars were burned. Proponents of the nationalism theory also point out that the border between the two countries was closed hours after the game.[96] Media in both countries began making accusations and counter-accusations of outrageous crimes, such as "woman stripped and violated in the street by Salvadoran mobs", genocide, and various forms of psychological degradation involving human feces and urine.[97] "Newspapers on both sides waged a campaign of hate, slander, and abuse, calling each other Nazis, dwarfs, drunkards, sadists, spiders, aggressors, and thieves".[98]

The OAS Human Rights Subcommittee reported "in the events which occurred in El Salvador and Honduras, the press and radio bear an enormous responsibility".[99] On July 17th, *The Washington Post* claimed that "the Salvadoreans living in Honduras are hostages to Honduran popular fury"[100] and again on July 18th

---

[94] Kapuściński, 158.

[95] Kapuściński, 158-159.

[96] Kapuściński, 158-159.

[97] Anderson, 94.

[98] Kapuściński, 183.

[99] Anderson, 101.

[100] "Central America's "Soccer War"." *The Washington Post* [Washington, D.C.] 17 July 1969: A14. Print.

reported from El Salvador that "A principal factor in the elevated passion both here and in Honduras has been incessant inflammatory broadcasts by both countries. The radio and most of the press have attacked without qualification each other's president, populace, and customs".[101] This issue became so important that the final peace treaty between the two countries even contained a specific article for mutual respect of people and culture and for ensuring responsible media in both countries.[102]

In the time of nationalist frenzy before the start of the war, the eviction of Salvadoran migrants became violent. Many Honduran civilians joined in the evictions as impromptu militias. Shops were burned and killings in rural areas occurred sporadically. Salvadoran newspapers made accusations of atrocities daily[103] while the Salvadoran government filed an official complaint with the Inter-American Commission on Human Rights.[104] When El Salvador formally severed diplomatic relations with Honduras on June 26th, the official justification given stated: "the government of Honduras has not taken any effective measures to punish these crimes which constitute genocide, nor has it given assurances of indemnification or reparations for the damages caused to Salvadoreans".[105] Honduras claimed the migrants were in the country illegally and that it was evicting the migrants under its own domestic laws regarding land rights.[106] The exact legality of evictions and the validity of accusations were lost in the media craze and subsequent outbreak of hostilities.

ASSESSING THE EVIDENCE AND THE PRIMARY CAUSE OF THE SOCCER WAR

It is evident that many of the predictions for each of the three theories were correct. The nationalism theory correctly predicted the

---

[101] Levy, Jack S., and William R. Thompson. *Causes of War*. Chichester, West Sussex, U.K.: Wiley-Blackwell, 2010. 211. Print.

[102] "GENERAL PEACE TREATY BETWEEN THE REPUBLICS OF EL SALVADOR AND HONDURAS." *United Nations Peacemaker*. United Nations, 17 Apr. 1980. Web. 13 Dec. 2013.

[103] Anderson, 96-101.

[104] Bachmura.

[105] Anderson, 105.

[106] Mundigo, 87.

occurrence of crimes based upon nationality, the assignment of collective blame by the public and each government, the occurrence of extensive, slanderous, and often false media coverage of these events, an unwillingness for repentance, and a lack of dissenting opinions in public discussion, with much of it focused on the migrants. This theory also predicts with a small degree of success discussions by leaders on both sides of crimes against the national honor, including genocide accusations, and the legal status of the migrants. It did not correctly predict national honor and prestige as the primary motivation for the use of force.

The overpopulation theory correctly predicted high population growth, high population density, insufficient domestic food production, and high landlessness. It failed to account for the ability of El Salvador to support its growing population with its given resources and incorrectly predicted a natural, as opposed to artificial, food shortage and overcrowding as the motivation for the migrants leaving El Salvador. Process tracing also does not support this theory. While it enhanced the problems posed by the land policies of both countries, it was not a primary factor in the decision-making process of El Salvador's leaders.

The land monopolization theory correctly predicted massive inequality in land ownership, mass landlessness, the domination of non-subsistence agriculture, and an artificial decline in food production. It incorrectly predicted social unrest related to landlessness and land inequality, though in the long term the subjugation of the peasant class during La Matanza cannot be ignored. A prediction of social unrest also appears to have been incorrect in and of itself, for social unrest was avoided through the displacement of the poor to Honduras. The migrants that did return to El Salvador, however, "erected shanty towns in San Salvador and on the edges of plantations, creating new pockets of social unrest".[107] Fears of the return of the migrants were well founded. The economic and agricultural data regarding El Salvador also points to the inability of El Salvador, with the land policies it had at the time, to accommodate the return of 300,000 migrants. Land policy drove the migrants from

---

[107] Barry, 111.

El Salvador and land policy prevented their return. There was no land available for them and hence no means of feeding them. The vast majority of crops being produced were for export and not domestic consumption.

Most importantly, process tracing strongly supports this theory. This theory correctly predicted Salvadoran leaders' fear of the landed elite and the resulting policy-making constraints this placed upon them. It also highlights their fears of the potential for social unrest if the migrants returned. Statements in the post-war victory speech by President Hernandez identify land as a major issue related to the war. Honduran politicians also repeatedly referenced the problem of land as it related to the issue of migrants and social unrest in El Salvador. Military planning also began a week before the first soccer match, when evictions were ongoing but before nationalist sentiment became virulent.

I conclude that land monopolization was the primary cause of the Soccer War, with overpopulation and nationalism serving as secondary causes. Land monopolization made the return of the migrants to El Salvador intolerable and their return a threat to the economic and political elite of the country. El Salvador was limited in the policy options it had available and thus had to resort to war.

GENERALIZABLE IMPLICATIONS: DISTANT AND PROXIMATE CAUSES AND FIRST-MOVE ADVANTAGES

The Soccer War provides a number of lessons that can be generalized to inter-state wars. It provides a clear demonstration of the benefits of utilizing a framework of distant and proximate causes of war. Levy and Thompson elaborate on this framework, stating that "in the aggregate, broad system-, economic-, or societal-level forces probably have a greater impact than particular individuals on the formation of rivalries and/or on the underlying processes leading to war, while the impact of individuals...usually increases as a dispute or crisis moves closer to final decisions for war".[108] All wars have multiple causes of varying importance. Some of these causes are

---

[108] Levy, Jack S., and William R. Thompson. *Causes of War*. Chichester, West Sussex, U.K.: Wiley-Blackwell, 2010. 211. Print.

distant and play out over the long-term. Others are proximate, affecting the likelihood of war in the short-term.

The economic and agricultural structures of colonization proved resilient over the course of Central American history. When the borders of Central America were drawn at the time of independence, El Salvador and Honduras gained resource endowments and economic and agricultural systems that set them on course for future tensions. Land policy steadily produced the circumstances that led to war, despite numerous opportunities to reform and such events as La Matanza. Land policy provided macro-level, long-term causes. Other causes are proximate and temporally close to the outbreak of war, such as the media war and consequent nationalist sentiment preceding the Soccer War in mid-June and early July of 1969. Individual politicians, landowners, and media personalities had more significant impact in this time period. Proximate and distant causes of war interact with one another in leading a given state to decide to go to war. Van Evera provides a general framework into which the primary cause of land monopolization and the secondary causes of nationalism and overpopulation interacted to increase the likelihood of war.

The Soccer War illustrates a clear case of Van Evera's hypothesis that war is more likely when the advantage lies with the first side to mobilize or attack.[109] In addition to a first-move advantage, other factors that may increase the risk of war identified by Van Evera applicable to the Soccer War include a preemptive first-strike and truncated diplomacy. Van Evera argues that a first-move advantage obtains when an attacker improves their prospect of victory through mobilizing and striking first. They may inflict greater damage on the other side than if they waited for the other side to attack them.

He also argues that a preemptive strike is likely when it is perceived to be likely that an opponent will strike first and obtain a first strike advantage. It is necessary to strike the opponent before they move first, in order to gain a first-strike advantage. Truncated diplomacy occurs when the benefits of obtaining a first-strike

---

[109] Van, Evera Stephen. "Jumping the Gun: First-Move Advantage and Crisis Instability." *Causes of War: Power and the Roots of Conflict.* Ithaca: Cornell UP, 1999. 35. Print.

advantage demand immediate action. Diplomacy may reduce the potential benefits of a first-strike advantage by consuming precious time. Thus diplomatic efforts are not fully pursued in order to obtain the maximum benefit of a first-strike advantage. As I have argued in this paper, land monopolization created the conditions that forced 300,000 Salvadorans into Honduras and made their return an imminent threat to El Salvador, necessitating the use of force. In the framework of Van Evera's first-move hypothesis, once faced with this imminent threat, El Salvador mobilized and struck first in order to obtain first-move advantages. War could not be avoided diplomatically because diplomacy was truncated.

El Salvador enjoyed a known advantage in ground forces, with approximately a 4 to 1 advantage in infantry. El Salvador could marshal an estimated 9,000 ground troops to Honduras' 2,500, widely known to be of lower quality than the Salvadoran forces. El Salvador also possessed superiority in artillery and small arms.[110] However, El Salvador was significantly weaker than Honduras in airpower. El Salvador possessed only 11 World War II-era combat aircraft. Honduras fielded 23 next-generation combat aircraft and had a known superiority in pilots. Honduras also possessed multiple airports capable of supporting military aircraft to El Salvador's one.[111] Both nations also positioned substantial numbers of troops on their shared border despite calls by the Central American Mediation Commission to demobilize on July 12th, presenting a situation in which there was a reciprocal fear of a surprise attack.

Van Evera's hypothesis correctly predicts the behavior of El Salvador on the three points presented here. First, Salvadoran leaders at the highest levels of government viewed the return of refugees as an imminent threat and sought a preemptive strike in order to prevent domestic insurrection or a coup. While the possibility of the fear of a Honduran surprise attack was possible, it was unlikely given the inferiority of the Honduran ground forces. That Honduras was aware of the threat posed to El Salvador by the return of the migrants was a more realistic possibility. Weiner has argued that forced population displacement can be an effective means of destabilizing a rival.[112]

---

[110] Anderson, 116.

[111] Anderson, 114.

[112] Weiner.

Regardless of intentions, the return of the migrants was perceived as an imminent threat.

Second, El Salvador sealed its border and severed diplomatic ties at the height of the crisis amidst a nationalistic frenzy, unable to attempt diplomacy for domestic reasons and greatly increasing the likelihood of war. Various Central American regional institutions, as well as the foreign ministers of several Central American nations, attempted to facilitate diplomacy between El Salvador and Honduras. The Honduran ambassador had also informed the Salvadoran government that the Honduran government was open to suggestions and that it did not wish to see violence. [113] Truncated diplomacy closed the door on a possible diplomatic resolution. It is also possible, given that military planning began on June 1st, that El Salvador would not have negotiated under any circumstances.

Third, El Salvador mobilized before Honduras on July 2nd, in anticipation of conflict and in the hope of striking first.[114] After 6 weeks of anticipating war in light of an imminent threat, El Salvador had multiple advantages to gain from a first-mobilization and a first-strike. El Salvador struck first in an attempt to nullify the air superiority of Honduras, striking at its airfields in the opening move of the assault. Surprise was achieved and the Salvadoran air assault proceeded to bomb multiple targets, including the Honduran capital, unopposed. In reference to this initial surprise air assault, Anderson finds that "The Salvadorans decided to overcome the enemy's advantage in equipment and training by launching a preemptive strike".[115] Its fears of the Honduran air force later proved to be correct, as Honduras counterattacked with its superior air force. The Honduran air force inflicted significant casualties on the Salvadoran air force and destroyed the main fuel storage sites of the Salvadoran ground forces. In failing to eliminate the Honduran air force, the superior Honduran air force was able to severely inhibit the movement of the superior Salvadoran ground forces. The motives to move first were validated by the events of the war. Had El Salvador

---

[113] Anderson, 108.

[114] Anderson, 108.

[115] Anderson, 114.

neutralized the Honduran air force, it likely would have won the war.[116] See Table 4 for a summary of the application of Van Evera's hypothesis to the Soccer War.

---

[116] Anderson, 115.

Table 4   Stephen Van Evera's First Move Hypothesis and the Soccer War

Preemptive Strike	First-Move Advantage	Truncated Diplomacy
Possible Reciprocal Fear of Surprise Attack Due to Honduran Mobilization	Mobilized First	Sealed Border
Imminent Threat of Migrant Return	Struck First in Undeclared Surprise Attack to Neutralize Honduran Air Force	Severed Diplomatic Ties

CONCLUSION

The Soccer War's primary cause was land monopolization. The wealthy elite of both El Salvador and Honduras held the political leaders of the two countries hostage and stymied every attempt at land reform, resorting to coups on multiple occasions. The civil war in El Salvador that began in 1980 was an extension of the unresolved land problems of the Soccer War.[117] The priorities of the wealthy have led to the continued denial of a means of survival to the majority of the population and led to multiple conflicts. A similar dynamic of inattentive and ignorant leaders fostered the collapse of the Maya in Central America, a far larger and, relative to time period, advanced civilization than El Salvador at the time of the Soccer War.[118] The needs of the majority of a given population cannot be ignored indefinitely. If elites do not address them, the masses will in time address them themselves.

Generalizable findings can also be derived from this case for inter-state war. This war provides evidence for Van Evera's first-move advantage hypothesis and the corollaries of preemptive strikes and truncated diplomacy. The issue of the migrants and of land policy in both countries could have been solved peacefully and war could have been avoided. Given the credence this case lends to Van Evera's

---

[117] Weinberg, 58.

[118] Diamond, Jared M. *Collapse: How Societies Choose to Fail or Succeed.* New York: Viking, 2005. 177. Print.

hypothesis, it may be possible to use this framework to identify similar situations in which the outbreak of war is likely and how it can be prevented.

In determining what a given state may identify as an imminent threat and in avoiding the truncation of diplomacy, the dynamics of a first-move advantage may not obtain. Effective inter-state communication regarding their national interests and what is acceptable and unacceptable for their security could significantly reduce the likelihood of war. In studying the causes of war, the causes of peace are also identified. It is these lessons that are valuable, for while the Soccer War may appear to be a structural inevitability; numerous opportunities for its prevention were missed.

African Education
Connor Chelsky

Education systems play an integral role in promoting a country's development, culture, and values. In order to reverse Western media portrayals that reduce Africa to a continent known only for starvation, conflict, and poverty, African nations must rely on strong public education systems. However, due to heavy dependency on Western aid, many countries are unable to implement policies that are organically conceived and relevant to those engaged in their education community. This is largely due to the intervention model used by donors that insist on tying their financial assistance to numerous conditions. In this paper, I argue that globalization and Western aid has a primarily negative effect on education policy and research funding in African countries due the cultural gentrification and aid dependency it generates.

The unwillingness of aid organizations to engage with the government and education actors of a state results in reform policies that even prominent members in the African country's education community cannot take ownership of due to their overwhelming foreign nature. This is attributed to reform policies being shaped almost exclusively by non-African researchers. Even when there is African involvement, it is often limited and constrained to the guidelines of the already established proposal. As a result, "those who are responsible for guiding and managing Africa's education systems do not regard these as *their* studies, developed for *their* benefit, and useful in *their* daily work"[119]. The lack of strong participation by national governments and their respective education communities in shaping the aim of such reform proposals leads researchers to address issues that are irrelevant to a majority of those engaged in the country's education sector. In addition, "nor [are]… results and recommendations organized and presented in ways that make them directly useful to education managers and administrators…. Principals, teachers, students, and parents see even less utility"[120]. By

---

[119] Samoff, p. 253
[120] Samoff, p. 255

opting for an intervention approach instead of forming local partnerships, aid organizations largely fail to produce reform policies that are relevant to populations their actions will affect the most.

The strong influence of foreign aid on the type and aim of research that occurs within the education sector of African countries leads to most research projects having short term, quick fix goals that fail to delve deeply into the complex issues facing many African education systems. Consulting with local education officials and spending extensive time at studied sites does not fit the short deadlines of most aid agencies. Instead, they resort to "short-order research based on brief visits that generate rapid results"[121]. The lack of time these researchers employed by such agencies are afforded produces research results that serve as a snapshot of an education system rather than comprehensive understanding that requires a long-term commitment. Consequently, this research often produces "sweeping conclusions with far-reaching ramifications"[122]. Researchers will continue to produce such recommendations until aid organizations allow researchers to operate without the strict time constraints under which they are currently imposed. The goals, methods, and the overwhelmingly foreign composition of these research teams must be dramatically changed if they are to create organic reform policies that participants in the education system throughout the country will view as legitimate.

Impoverished African countries have developed a dependence on aid organizations such as the World Bank and other Western powers to develop education reform measures that involve everything from textbook choices to curriculum formation. In his article on the education sector in Africa, Samoff writes, "Where public funding for education is inadequate, public funding for education research hardly exists…scholars look abroad for support for their research."[123] Therefore, African governments and researchers must often submit to the framework and goals of the aid agencies if they are to obtain funding for research at all. This presents a myriad of problems including: "devalu[ing] the local role…legitimizing weak propositions; entrenching flawed understandings by according them official status"[124]. In addition, World Bank reports that discouraged

---

[121] Samoff, p. 256
[122] Samoff, p. 255
[123] Samoff, p. 257

the investment in African higher education for a time have had a significant effect on the quality of higher education in Africa. Lower rates of investment led to a greater "dependence of Africa on studies overseas… employing expatriates in African institutes of higher learning and with nationals who… have been given most western concepts and research methodologies"[125]. Due the control of aid organizations over the type and subject of research that is conducted on African education systems, there is a significant dearth of organic education research sponsored solely by African governments or institutions.

The results that are published with African government approval and by African researchers appear to have more legitimacy and utility to outside observers, but the numerous restrictions placed on these researchers do not allow them to conduct projects with the freedom necessary to produce reports that are truly indicative of the local situation and able to offer the population utility. Oftentimes, "government officials… are apparently reluctant to assert more firmly their own concerns and interests for fear of jeopardizing continued or new foreign funding"[126]. If aid agencies are to sponsor research efforts, they must allow local researchers to conduct projects free of restrictions that inhibit the local input and long-term analysis needed to produce high quality results. However, in order to truly reduce dependence and create competition, national governments must invest in education research projects that their academic communities can proudly claim as their own--projects that can be used to better inform local policymakers when attempting to establish important components of a nation's education agenda.

The quality of research regarding education should be of the utmost importance, due to the critical importance educational systems have on a nation's development. However, by relying on foreign funding to sponsor education researchers and reform efforts, African countries become increasingly dependent on foreign aid. The elimination of debt is highly preferable to the continuation of loans because of the profound impact dependence can have in this case[127] In

[124] Samoff, p. 257
[125] Banya & Elu, p. 25
[126] Samoff, p. 264

addition, "one NGO activist noted the link between debt relief and education in pointing out 'it has been going to the construction of classroom… and this made available infrastructure and learning materials'"[128]. If allowed greater financial autonomy and responsibility, states can fund their own research regarding education systems and create their own reform policies based on the issues that local educators believe are important. By providing a greater education system for their citizens, states can reap the benefits of gained trust and support. If they do not appropriate funds well and their education system fails, political leaders will be held directly responsible[129]. Aid agencies, according to Moyo, allow corrupt policymakers to partake in financially irresponsible activities free from repercussions. However, if it is the money of the nation's taxpayers being spent frivolously on luxurious shopping trips or automobiles for the political elite instead of education, the people will rise up and remove the leader from power. This intolerance of corruption would set a precedent for future persons of power to invest state funds responsibly, creating greater efficiency and ownership over state actions.

The influence of Western powers also has a strong impact on the cultural components of African education due to the variety of conditions that are attached to aid packages. This Western influence is primarily seen in aspects of education such as curriculum development, language of instruction, and textbook providers. The issue of colonial powers exerting control over major education policies has often been present since the 1960s, when many African states were newly independent. Such influence was made possible because states were often concerned with discerning the logistics of providing public education for large percentages of the population that had previously been denied access. Consequentially, "while the African educationists were busy fulfilling the promise of schooling for the African masses, the curriculum and textbooks, along with teaching methods were in the hands of the educational industry and publishers of the North."[130] Due to the lack of resources and capability to handle the immense task of creating and operating a new

---

[127] Moyo
[128] Wood, p. 202
[129] Moyo
[130] Brock-Utne, p. 179

education system, countries such as Kenya had to rely on curriculum packages developed by their former colonizers. For example, the development of the New Primary Approach (NPA) was developed and managed in Kenya with British money and personnel.

These imported programs and curricula caused numerous cultural and logistical problems, creating "widespread dissatisfaction among teachers and students… of which great parts are irrelevant for a largely agrarian population like in Kenya."[131] Not only was the curriculum irrelevant for significant percentages of the Kenyan population, the NPA program also dictated that primary students must study it in English. This foreign developed policy completely ignored "the problem of first language interference and the effect of the new approach on the pupil's self-confidence."[132] The cultural gentrification and suboptimal learning environments produced by such policies inhibits African education systems from making substantial strides in quality needed to improve long term development.

The attitudes of Western powers toward African states exacerbates the dependence of African countries on foreign aid. This dependence has continued the practice of strong colonial influence on education policy decisions made by African governments. A study by the World Bank in 1990 displayed:

> "That in most cases educational projects in the South have been designed and are now increasingly coordinated by donor agencies in the North, not by national governments in developing countries, and certainly not by their local population. Projects are tied to deliveries of equipment and key personnel from the donor country and, generally, only to a minor extent to the full utilization of local expertise and supplies."[133]

The creation and implementation of educational projects without input from the national government, let alone the local population, is a strong example of the detrimental effects of foreign aid discussed by

---

[131] Brock-Utne, p. 180
[132] Brock-Utne, p. 180
[133] Brock-Utne, p. 184

Moyo in her novel *Dead Aid*. The presumption that these African countries and their citizens are unable or unfit to create successful education programs for their own population presumes a helplessness or inferiority that is incredibly demeaning.

The dependence of African countries on foreign aid has made them highly sensitive to the increasing demands and conditions Western countries place on aid. These conditions often contain aspects that do not fulfill the specific needs of the state or examine the local context in which their programs will be applied. Language of instruction, in particular, is subject to the whims of donors. For example, despite Somali being the language of instruction in primary and secondary schools in Somalia, university level courses are taught primarily in Italian. Despite Italian not being a studied language taught at lower levels, "the choice of Italian has been decided by the fact that Italy is the donor giving development aid, including both lecturers and text-books, to most of the faculties at the University."[134] Such inefficiencies could easily be solved through greater cooperation with local education experts, allowing aid dollars to be better utilized. Instead, by forcing language requirements on recipient countries, donors gradually erode local and national languages that are critical components of a nation's culture.

Inefficiencies created by disregard for local language and culture fail to take into account the educational practices of the country and create barriers to student achievement that are ultimately detrimental to a country's development. Despite having its own national language, Madagascar switched the language of instruction in secondary school to French due to their reliance on aid from France, who provided the country textbooks "as a type of educational aid"[135]. Even countries that have demonstrated capability to publish their own textbooks have suffered from decisions made by aid organizations. For example, the World Bank decided the "local development and production of school textbooks by the National Pedagogical Institute in Mali (IPN) was too expensive... textbooks are now being developed by EDICEF in France or Tunisia."[136] Not only are some children subjected to being taught in a second language, but now are also subjected to a curriculum that is largely irrelevant. This is of little concern to

---

[134] Brock-Utne, p. 186
[135] Brock-Utne, p. 186
[136] Brock-Utne, p. 185

Northern publishing companies, however, "which profit directly from the continued use or reintroduction of the colonial languages in the schools in Africa."[137] By deeming local textbook production, which supports "the publication of other books… and the intellectual life of a country", as unimportant, donors reduce the value of children receiving education in the context of their local and national culture that best fits their learning needs[138]. The conflict of interest that is raised by former colonial powers profiting off of projects labeled as aid is irresponsible, unethical, and diminishes the value of aid given by donor countries.

The creation of international standards used to evaluate the quality of education systems is another form of donor intervention that could negatively impact African countries. Such international standards could eventually lead to a global form of tests and curriculum imposed on aid dependent countries by their respective donors. These measures would undoubtedly be overwhelmingly influenced by approaches developed by Western experts, endangering national curriculums established by African countries. Already significant levels of cultural conditionality present in aid terms would increase in response to internationally manufactured testing. In order to prevent such cultural corrosion from occurring, projects would have to heed the words of Danish educational researcher Spaet Henriksen, who said, "It would not be possible to embark on a project which defines itself as 'help to self-helping' without trying to understand as much as possible of the culture of the country, its history and the structure and content of its education"[139]. Failure to do so could lead to serious detrimental effects on the indigenous culture of African nations that the global community should seek to preserve in order to avoid the potential erosion of both local and national culture..

Foreign aid programs that approach relationships with African countries and universities as equal partnerships instead of traditional unbalanced donor-recipient relationships are able to benefit both parties much more effectively. By implementing programs that are founded on an equal exchange of knowledge, scholars and education

---

[137] Brock-Utne, p. 186
[138] Brock-Utne, p. 185
[139] Henriksen, p. 71

experts in both partner countries can learn from each other. Not only would such a system have greater utility for both parties, it would also remove the demeaning aspect present in programs that focus on a one sided transfer of knowledge. One example of such a program is the "ALLEX programme… a joint project of the universities of Zimbabwe, Gothenburg and Oslo to provide a range of monolingual dictionaries for the local languages in Zimbabwe… the project is a major step in upgrading some African languages for the benefit of local people."[140] Not only does this program employ local Zimbabweans, but the Swedish and Norwegian scholars benefit as well. In return for their work, "Swedish and Norwegian lexicographers are taught about structures in African languages they did not know before and about meanings… rooted in a different cultural setting."[141] The ALLEX program was well received by Zimbabweans due to this equal exchange method. Besides the gains made by all parties, a particular success of the program was the strengthening of Zimbabwean culture through aiding efforts to preserve and encourage local languages. By sharing their experience and technology used to construct dictionaries, the ALLEX program is an exemplary model of the benefits globalization can have on African education systems and culture.

The delivery model primarily utilized by aid organizations in African countries is inefficient, degrading, and outdated. As Dambisa Moyo emphasizes throughout her book *Dead Aid*, loans and interventions modeled after programs employed by the Marshall Plan have experienced minimal, if any, success in promoting sustainable development in the continent. Instead, according to Moyo, aid has "hampered, stifled and retarded Africa's development"[142] This perpetuation of poverty, slow growth, and corruption has hindered the ability of national governments in Africa to personally develop and fund their own education systems. Wallowing in debt produced by international loans, education programs are often first in line to experience budgetary cuts. Consequentially, when aid organizations step in to help fund these financially stricken education system, policymakers have little choice but to agree to whatever terms donors set or risk being unable to keep schools open at all. As seen in

[140] Brock-Utne, p. 192
[141] Brock-Utne, p. 188
[142] Moyo, p. 9

previously mentioned examples, donors often implement measures without significant input from the local education community. As a result, serious issues arise in areas such as language of instruction, relevance of textbooks, and context of curriculum. Left unattended, such problems have the potential to have severely negative impacts a country's economic development and continued presence of treasured local cultures.

Aid organizations must adopt the approaches of programs such as ALLEX that have experienced success due to components such as cooperation, equal exchange of information, and significant local involvement. The greater relevancy and cultural integration present in such programs allows everyone from education experts to local teachers to identify and appreciate the research and reform measures produced by such partnerships. While Moyo argues for an immediate and total elimination of systemic aid to Africa, in terms of aid to education systems and research it would be more beneficial to take a more gradual approach to eliminating aid dependency. Block grants and aid with no strings attached can have positive effects and allow for greater investment in education[143]. In addition, countries that have been offered debt relief have used those saved funds to invest in their education systems. Allowing countries and academic experts to take responsibility for the successes or failures of their education systems will provide domestic policymakers greater ownership over the support or disapproval that results from their actions.

Education systems are instrumental in efforts to foster sustainable development, cultural pride, and a stable society. Ruling political parties such as SWAPO in Namibia have used education to help to counter past effects of apartheid, arguing, "People come first, and basically people cannot be 'developed' – they can only develop themselves."[144] The assumption that foreign aid agencies can successfully implement education policy without significant involvement of local experts, based on research projects and recommendations universally disowned by a country's education community, is absurd. This model not only belittles the ability of the African people, but also keeps Africa "in its perpetual childlike state"[145]

---

[143] Brautigam
[144] Fumanti, p. 89

. By refusing to treat Africans as equals, aid agencies have cultivated a dependency that is counterproductive to successful, organic reform. By abandoning archaic practices and adopting a more cooperative partnership approach, aid organizations can better support the efforts of African countries attempting to achieve sustainable development and empowerment with the establishment of a quality education system compatible with national values and culture.

[145] Moyo p. 32

References

Banya, K., and J. Elu. The world bank and financing higher education in sub-saharan africa. *HIGHER EDUCATION; High.Educ.* 42 (1): 1-34.

Brautigam, Deborah. 2009. *The dragon's gift : The real story of china in africa*Oxford England ; New York : Oxford University Press.

BROCKUTNE, B. Cultural conditionality and aid to education in east- africa. *INTERNATIONAL REVIEW OF EDUCATION; Int.Rev.Educ.* 41 (3-4): 177-97.

Fumanti, Mattia. Nation building and the battle for consciousness: Discourses on education in post-apartheid namibia.(SPECIAL SECTION). *Social Analysis* 50 (3): 84.

Henriksen, S.1993. *Thoughts about "action competence" in the cultural meeting with*

Lithuania. In: Jensen, B.B. and Karsten Schnack, eds., *action competence* as a

didactical concept. Copenhagen: *Didaktiske studier.*70-75

Moyo, Dambisa. 2009. *Dead aid : Why aid is not working and how there is a better way for africa*New York : Farrar, Straus and Giroux.

Samoff, Joel. 1999. Education sector analysis in africa: Limited national control and even less national   ownership. *International Journal of Educational Development* 19 (4): 249-72

Wood, Jane C. Millar. 2008. *The impact of globalization on education reform a case study of Uganda.* College Park, Md.: University of Maryland.

Fides Quaerens Intellectum:
Notre Dame and the Revival of the University in America
Katelyn Doering

If the Catholic university can fulfill this first function of the human mind seeking faith ... it will indeed be a great light in the all-encompassing darkness that engulfs our world today.
- Fr. Theodore M. Hesburgh, C.S.C.

No one who sets foot on the campus of the University of Notre Dame can deny that there is something special about this university, its physical environment and its people. As Lou Holtz famously said, "If you've been there, no explanation is necessary. If you haven't, no explanation will suffice." There is a reason that students love this sentiment and so frequently re-quote it. They wholeheartedly understand the feeling that no explanation will suffice.

My conviction that Notre Dame is different was confirmed by an article in *Notre Dame Magazine* last summer, titled "Where do you stand?" The article, written by Professor O'Callaghan in the Philosophy department, details the history of the iconic layout of God Quad and explores the connections between the University's physical space and its unique mission. Inspired by the sight of a student tour guide standing with her back to the *"Venite ad me omnes"* statue of Christ, O'Callaghan meditates on how the expansion away from the "heart of campus" reflects a deeper, more troubling shift in the University's mission and focus. He does not deny the University its right to grow; on the contrary, he argues that growth was necessary in order that Father Sorin's project might "be true to the promise within Notre Dame to embody the genuine character of a university."[i] However, he expresses concern over the nature and effects of this growth: "And yet, will the intellectual growth of the University obscure from it the truth that makes it truly great ... ? Will Notre Dame, like the tour guide, turn its back to Christ?"[ii]

This concern over a shift in focus at Notre Dame is part of a much broader societal problem plaguing America. Intellectual trends have gradually abandoned the classical model of the university, in which scholars act as an organic whole whose mission is centered around the pursuit of truth. By contrast, the modern university is a research-based, individualized collection of scholars, united by little more than the shared physical spaces of their campus. The evolution of democratic society as described by Alexis de Tocqueville in *Democracy in America* is reflected through the lens of the status of the modern university.

I will outline the difference between aristocratic and democratic social patterns as Tocqueville presents them. I will then explore a specific aspect of these concepts, namely, Tocqueville's argument about the trends in intellectual life which occur over time in democratic societies. I will then apply this theory to the status of the modern university and argue that the American university's observable departure from the traditional character of the university is symptomatic of the increased democratization of American society that Tocqueville predicts. Finally, I develop the claim that a Catholic university like Notre Dame has a unique role to play in reversing this trend, both by virtue of its role as a university and its Catholic identity.

The Meaning of "Aristocracy" and "Democracy" in Tocqueville

In *Democracy in America,* Tocqueville develops a contrast between the kinds of social relationships in "aristocratic" and "democratic" societies. Throughout Tocqueville's argument, these labels derive their descriptive power primarily from the animating social patterns and manners of thinking that he observes in these societies. These separate patterns produce two kinds of individuals with very different conceptions of relationship: to self, to community, to material objects, and to time and place.

An aristocratic individual's concept of self is primarily defined by his or her relationship to others. There is a strong sense of the importance of tradition, and people look at the past with gratitude. There is also an animating sense of duty. Strong ties to physical places and a sense of obligation to the future makes the stewardship of family, possessions, and legacy an important priority. Aristocratic societies tend to elevate the beautiful and the durable, building homes and artifacts to last.

By contrast, a democratic individual is self-created and resists being defined by relationships. The belief that claims imposed by the past and the future are arbitrary leads people in democratic societies to devalue duty in favor of rights. Equality is a primary virtue in a democratic society. A focus on the present severs ties to place and contributes to great social and physical mobility. These democratic emphases tend to lead people to produce buildings, clothing, and objects that have a more utilitarian purpose.

The Decline into Democratic Intellectualism

Having established this contrast between aristocracy and democracy, Tocqueville goes on to present a number of ways in which a democratic society is prone to a descent into its most fundamental characteristics. To illustrate his point, he describes many American institutions, such as the Christian religion, the family, the worker's union, and the university. As a product of aristocratic social patterns, each of these institutions has an "aristocratic character" that preserves ties to others within society, carving out a place for the individual. Nevertheless, as Tocqueville claims, a regime with mixed elements of democracy and aristocracy can ultimately only be defined as one or the other; a truly mixed society is a chimera, a fictional creature.[iii] Despite the presence of aristocratic influences, America is driven by democratic animating principles that will gradually manifest themselves and eventually predominate.

One of the most salient effects of these democratic tendencies, and the one most relevant to the intellectual life, is the fragmentation of society into a homogenous group of atomized individuals. Each citizen in a democratic society will ultimately prefer to retreat, as Tocqueville puts it, into the "solitude of his own heart."[iv] He will pull away from the institutions and the generational connections present in aristocratic ages, the connections that tie him to a particular place and present him with a duty to the past and the future. The principle of equality drives this fragmentation of society. Individuals in democratic society will resent the distinctions that aristocratic institutions and connections create. Thus, they will fight to diminish the influence of these intermediary structures until, gradually, none of the institutions preserve the aristocratic character or occupy the prominent position that they once did. The only thing holding the society together in this democratic end-state is the citizens' economic interest and the benevolent bureaucratic regime which will ultimately assume all responsibility for the smooth functioning of society.

As in myriad other aspects of Tocqueville's America, this individualizing process is evident in American intellectual life. The American philosophical approach is one in which citizens reject tradition as anything more than a source of historical information in favor of the process of "seek[ing] by themselves and in themselves for the only reason for things."[v] This is a philosophical environment dependent on individual contemplation in which "each man is narrowly shut up in himself, and from that basis makes the pretension to judge the world."[vi] Members of society share no philosophical connections to each other on an ideological level since "each man undertakes to be sufficient to himself"; each citizen refuses to exclude beliefs as invalid and instead allows each of his neighbors to develop his own plan of life using his own judgment. As a result, "No longer do ideas, but interests only, form the links between men."[vii]

According to Tocqueville, the tyranny of majority opinion directly follows from this dependence on individual thought. The majority in a democratic society will hold sway over the social realm as well as the political realm, governing not just policy decisions but also extending its authority to customs and moral opinion. Tocqueville discusses the power that majority opinion holds over individual thought, concluding that "I know no country in which, speaking generally, there is less independence of mind and true freedom of discussion than in America."[viii] He argues that this is a negative development for America since it is more conducive to the eventual political tyranny of the despotic super-state.

In his *The Closing of the American Mind*, Allan Bloom expands on Tocqueville's argument, pointing out the paradox of dependent patterns of thought:

> Although every man in democracy thinks himself individually the equal of every other man, this makes it difficult to resist the collectivity of equal men. ... This is the really dangerous form of the tyranny of the majority, not the kind that actively persecutes minorities but the kind that breaks the inner will to resist because there is no qualified source of nonconforming principles and no sense of superior right.[ix]

Both Bloom and Tocqueville argue that this kind of intellectual tyranny is detrimental to true democracy as they understand it. A society that expects every individual to develop his own philosophy of life will result in little actual diversity of thought. In a democratic society, citizens' focus on their private economic activities leaves them little time for such a task of self-reflection. Bloom further implies that the lack of a "sense of superior right" is ultimately harmful to the intellectual community because it destroys connections to universal questions and answers that enrich a society's intellectual tradition and its search for improvement. Taken together, Tocqueville's observations about American intellectual trends are consistent with his more general conclusions about the end-state of American democracy.

The Crisis of the University in America

The increasingly democratic trend in America corresponds to the evolution of the modern university. Several aspects of the modern university illuminate this trend: the specialization of research; the emphasis on applied over theoretical knowledge; and the reluctance to embrace the pursuit of objective truth as its primary mission.

While an ancient university was understood as a group of scholarly people working to serve the same ends, a modern university is a collection of scholarly people working to serve different ends. Instead of seeing his or her work as part of an organic whole and seeking to identify common threads between dissimilar disciplines, a modern scholar builds a lifetime career around pursuing a highly specialized subsection of a field in order to make one small but very deep contribution to a larger body of academic work. Scholars at a modern university see this fragmentation of ends as a positive outcome of research specialization. In his essay "The Research Ideal," Anthony Kronman explores the theory initiated by the first professional academics in the nineteenth century. Academic specialization, much like economic specialization, promotes greater quality and quantity of work as part of a continuity over time. Ultimately, the work of many scholars will produce a clearer picture of the discipline studied. Furthermore, these academics, especially Max Weber, saw the devotion to a particular specialized area of study as a vocation, a scholar's duty to pursue in order to fulfill the particular task assigned to him. Seeking connections between many disciplines and building general knowledge about many topics would serve no meaningful purpose and would waste the scholar's intellectual potential. In a modern university, the effects of research specialization can be clearly seen in the huge variety of original research performed by its faculty, the use of highly technical language not easily understood by experts in other disciplines, and the importance of published research to the tenure process. None of these tendencies correspond with the idea of a university as an organic whole.

The modern university, unlike its predecessors, places increased emphasis on applied knowledge and devalues theoretical contributions. According to Tocqueville's explanation of democratic values, this observed tendency corresponds to the general tendency of a democratic society to value practicality and usefulness over all other defining features of buildings, clothing and goods. Bloom adds academic knowledge to Tocqueville's list of elements which become increasingly practical in democratic societies. He claims that "the democratic concentration on the useful, on the solution of what are believed by the populace at large to be the most pressing problems, makes theoretical distance seem not only useless but immoral."[x] The modern university focuses on the practical applications of knowledge it wishes to transmit to students. It is not worth understanding the meaning of life if this knowledge produces nothing tangible and useful; beyond a certain threshold of inquiry, it becomes no longer necessary to pursue the meaning of life for its own sake. Evidence of this trend is found in the modern university's emphasis on science, technology, engineering and math (STEM) achievement, the ever-present concerns about career paths and service work, and the fear expressed by students that a liberal arts degree in philosophy or English will fail to provide employable skills.

Lastly, the modern university departs from tradition in that it eschews the need to declare the pursuit of a particular truth, or even that of truth at all, as part of its animating and unifying mission. The great American universities were founded on religious principles, and the education they offered existed for a theological purpose. The model of the classical university was the idea of one in which a particular kind of student was formed. The term "professor" shares a root with the term "profess," indicating that a professor exemplifies some unified truth or coherent belief and cares about passing it on to his or her students. By contrast, the modern university is reluctant to establish a particular conception of the truth and promulgate it as a unified body. This tendency is in keeping with a democracy's tendency to discount authorities that claim to hold objectively true beliefs. Professors at a modern university choose to profess nothing more than the idea that everyone may discern the truth for himself. More direct evidence of the trend away from establishment of truth is found in many schools' rejection of their Latin mottos in favor of more modern mission statements focused around exploration, progress, and choice. When examining these characteristics together with those caused by other aspects of the democratic intellectual age, we see a modern model of the university that is both incredibly conformed to the democratic lifestyle and far distant from its original character as a "university," literally a "universal" institution of learning.

The Catholic University's Answer

The democratization and modernization of the university is a troublesome outcome worthy of reversal both because it has deleterious effects on the purest forms of academic inquiry such as philosophy and because it plunges a society further into democratic degradation and closer to democratic despotism. The Tocquevillian university serves as an important moderating force through its connections to the past and its promotion of independent thought in a society that rejects both. A society without stable institutions of an aristocratic character, according to Tocqueville, cannot last long as a democracy of free people who live up to their fullest potential as citizens. Any decline in the university causes citizens to lose the important opportunity, in the words of Bloom, to have "experiences they cannot have" in a democratic society, experiences that provide a powerful alternative to the democratic view of how they should see the world and their humanity.[xi] Clearly, in order to preserve democracy in its truest form, we must preserve the aristocratic nature of the university.

While Protestant universities have lost their original motivating ethos, Catholic universities have not escaped this fate. Despite exemplifying the elements of Tocqueville's "aristocratic character," the Catholic university is still very much at risk of becoming a part of the surrounding academic climate rather than daring "to be different in making a difference."[xii] If the work of restoring the university is to be carried out, it is imperative that Catholic universities join this work. By virtue of its Catholic character, the Catholic university brings a unique perspective to the work of returning American intellectual life to its roots.

This perspective is seen in the attributes of Catholicism which mitigate democratic despotism, namely, the value it places on memory and natural distinctions, as well as those attributes which are conducive to democracy in its truest form, especially the Church's clear articulation of the concept of human dignity. These attributes combine in the Catholic understanding to allow a unique view both of democracy's downfalls and of the goals of the university properly understood. The ethos of the university and the ethos of the Church form an ideal combination that fosters true inquiry about the human good and defends the human person against those forces that seek to isolate him.

A Catholic university's, or any university's, mission is about memory. A university preserves knowledge, tradition, and patterns of question and answer in a way that few other institutions can. Among these few others is the Roman Catholic Church. Theologians, saints, priests, and lay people have passed along important points of doctrine and important questions of the faith for centuries. The Catholic's understanding of his or her connectedness to time helps a Catholic university to better understand that a university should embody this connectedness.

A university is also a place to study natural distinctions. Classifying the defining attributes of people, nations, and elements of the natural environment – not just on the surface but on the most fundamental levels – is a concern that permeates all traditions of academic study. It is one of the techniques that nearly all disciplines share. The doctrine of the Catholic Church and the Christian faith in general is likewise deeply rooted in the study of distinctions. The creation accounts in Genesis celebrate the differences between the animal and the human, as only the latter are made in God's image.

The Catholic theology of the body celebrates the unique contributions of male and female to human relationships and society. From the most basic articulations of the faith, the Creeds, we find a detailed description of who God is and how he is distinct from the rest of His creation. Democracy wishes to eliminate all distinctions, even those between these seemingly immutable categories; theories of the personhood of animals and natural objects, feminism and the culture wars, and pantheist religious movements are all evidence of this trend. In light of this opposition of aristocratic and democratic claims, the Catholic understanding of natural distinction serves two purposes. It makes the rightful mission of the university more evident, and it fights this democratic tendency to blur the lines of the created order into homogeneity.

Certain characteristics of the Catholic view of the human person are especially compatible both with the mission of the classical university and with democracy in its truest form. The Catholic Church is a champion of human dignity, refusing to regard any person as less of a human being because of his or her distinctions. Instead, the Church chooses to see the person both as a unique individual and as a crucial part of the grand group of humanity, worthy of celebration in both capacities. The Catholic ethos of human dignity is deeply rooted in the most fundamental doctrines of Christianity. It can truly inform the way a university studies questions of the nature of the human person and his ends of life, as well as preserving the free individual in a democratic society that wishes to atomize him into insignificance. It is also compatible with the democratic tendency to view all humankind with the same benevolent, concerned gaze.

In summary, Catholicism both finds ways to combat the more detrimental effects of democratic degradation and to support the democratic tendencies which sustain a free people. These efforts are helpful both in restoring the true role of the university and in restoring the democratic character of the society. As Father Hesburgh puts it: "The Catholic university does have something spectacular to offer, ... a belief in an ultimate goal surpassing all natural endeavor. The Catholic university must be all that a university requires and something more."[xiii]

Notre Dame Seeking a Way Forward

Thus, Notre Dame finds itself at the center of a crisis it did not choose, with an obligation to reverse the trend before the modern university and American democratic society become unrecognizable. Regardless of the way in which Notre Dame chooses to begin this process of renewal, it is imperative that some steps be taken. The restoration of the ideal of the university means great things both for academia and for the health of American democracy. What is more, Our Lady's University is too special a place to outgrow its mission, lose sight of the true calling of a university, and, in the words of O'Callaghan, turn its back on Christ.

---

[i] John O'Callaghan, "Where do you stand?", *Notre Dame Magazine,* Summer 2012, 4.

[ii] O'Callaghan, "Where do you stand?", 5.

[iii] Alexis de Tocqueville, *Democracy in America* (New York: Harper & Row, 1969), 251.

[iv] Tocqueville, *Democracy,* 508.

[v] Tocqueville, *Democracy,* 429.

[vi] Tocqueville, *Democracy,* 430.

[vii] Tocqueville, *Democracy,* 432-3.

[viii] Tocqueville, *Democracy,* 255.

[ix] Allan Bloom, "Tocqueville on Democratic Intellectual Life," in *The Closing of the American Mind* (New York: Simon and Schuster, 1987), 247.

[x] Bloom, "Tocqueville," 250.

[xi] Bloom, "Tocqueville," 256.

[xii] O'Callaghan, "Where do you stand?", 6.

[xiii] Theodore M. Hesburgh, C.S.C., "The Vision of the Catholic University in the World of Today," in *The Hesburgh Papers: Higher Values in Higher Education* (Kansas City: Andrews and McMeel, Inc., 1979), 48.

Education in Rural Colombia:
Assessing its Contribution to State-Building and Formation of Democratic Citizens

Ilse Zenteno

Introduction

In the midst of the ongoing peace talks between the State of Colombia and the FARC — a guerrilla group called Fuerzas Armadas Revolucionarias de Colombia, translated as the Revolutionary Armed Forces of Colombia — which began in November of 2012, it is imperative to investigate how exactly the State hopes to gain legitimacy and citizen support in its conflict-ridden rural areas. This is an aspect in which the State of Colombia has been incapable of or unwilling to meet the demands of its local communities. Inadequate or nonexistent public services and insufficient economic opportunities have plagued these areas for generations. In turn, other actors, such as the FARC, have come to juxtapose their own authority over that of the State. In this climate of insecurity and state capture by illegal forces, Colombia's children and education system have come to be firmly under siege. Scholar Phil Price explained, "Boys and girls as young as thirteen are pulled out of classrooms and thrown into battlefields. Teachers routinely disappear and/or are subjected to extrajudicial executions. Guerillas, paramilitaries, and the Colombian army all utilize school buildings as posts for their combatants. School zones have become littered with landmines. Child displacement and poverty have reached endemic levels."[i] As it has been noted, "Education provision played a vital role in the early years of state-building in Europe by establishing legitimacy and citizen support, and fostering civic virtue and nationalism (Hobbsbawn 1990, Gellner 1983; B. Anderson 1983; Laitin 1877; Latin 1998; Weber 197)."[ii] In this essay, I will begin by giving a brief historical overview of the conflict and then analyze Colombia's public education system, as well as that of the FARC's, assessing their contributions to both state-building and forming democratic citizens.

Synopsis of the Conflict in Colombia

After its independence from Spain in 1817, Colombia continued its colonial legacy of exploiting and marginalizing the poor. An elite-two party system solidified; land and capital consolidated in the hands of a few. And yet, in the 1940s, landed elites sought to further "modernize" the Colombian economy — increase their crop revenues on coffee, a leading export. To do so, landlords induced a "large-scale population movement out of the countryside" and into the cities.[iii] Settlers and tenant farmers reacted and resisted. Tension between the upper and lower classes intensified, until in 1948, a civil war period known as *la violencia* exploded. After ten gory years, over 200,000 people lay dead.[iv] In 1958, "the populist threat eventually pushed the ruling classes to unite, forming the 'National Front' in which the two traditional parties" — the Liberals and the Conservatives — agreed to share power.[v] In 1964, peasants still resisting the government formed the FARC. In response, paramilitaries funded by landlords, drug cartels, and other economic interests emerged. Due to the State's incapacity to fulfill specific economic, social, and cultural obligations or guarantee personal security, there is still no peace to this day.[vi]

Today, poverty and inequality still exist. According to the Gini Index, land concentration in Colombia increased in the last decade from 0.74 to 0.87.[vii] Moreover, 20% of Colombians claim 60% of the national income.[viii] According to the International Fund for Agricultural Development, 46% of its 47 million people live in poverty (as of 2009); in rural areas, more than 7 million people are poor and 2 million live in extreme poverty.[ix] Furthermore, for the fourth year in a row, Colombia, with its estimated 4.9 to 5.5 million internally displaced people, tops the Norwegian Refugee Council's Internal Displacement Monitoring global list.[x] As has been evidenced, it is rural Colombia that has been most violently affected by this six-decade long conflict.

Education in Rural Colombia

In rural Colombia, public education has often been neglected, mismanaged, or under-resourced. Sometimes "only five years of primary school may be offered, although primary education for children between six and 12 years old and a total of nine years of education are free and compulsory."[xi] Furthermore, whereas literacy may be close to universal and net coverage in the primary grades may not be far behind in urban cities, the picture is completely different in rural areas. According to Adriana González, Coordinator of the Rural Education Program from Colombia's Ministry of Education, "rural areas had illiteracy rates of 19.5% in 2005, and test scores in math, language, and science among rural students lagged two to three percent behind those of their urban counterparts."[xii] Especially in coffee-growing regions, school attendance is troublesome: while the primary net attendance rate is similar in urban and rural areas, with 91.5% and 89%, respectively, secondary net attendance rate declines dramatically in rural regions, 48.3%, compared with 76.2% in urban areas.[xiii] Additionally, "only 69% of secondary school-age children in Colombia are actually in school, and just 30% of the urban students and 16% of rural students complete their basic education."[xiv] However, according to a forum that sought to bring together public and private actors in providing education to these rural areas, "these high dropout rates indicate that youth and their families do not find education relevant to their needs and daily lives."[xv] However, an overwhelming amount of research indicated that in these regions, it has been "the failure of local authorities in many places to provide sufficient schools and adequately staff them with teachers — whether for sheer lack of resources, inefficiency, or outright corruption."[xvi]

The Role of the State: Juntas Accíon de Comunal

While the State has sought to implement development projects in much of these rural areas, their intentions — at least previously — had been more political than of actually wanting to reform the rural education system. In 1958, for example, in response to *la violencia* and the rising social unrest due to the National Front's political exclusion and brewing of communist ideologies in the countryside, the State sought to mitigate tensions through a localized development strategy known as the Juntas Accíon de Comunal (Community Action Boards, or JACs). Funded by the state, JACs were organized by rural subdivisions and urban neighborhoods. They focused on constructing schools, clinics, and roads, along with the extensions of water and sewer lines. However, because they were "completely guided by state-based development officials and the dominant class," JACs "rejected local input."[xvii] Opposing Amartya Sen's perspective of *development as freedom,* the people were not seen "as being actively involved — given the opportunity — in shaping their own destiny;" on the contrary, they were seen as "passive recipients of the fruits of cunning development programs."[xviii] Indeed, the main goal of the JACs was not to "alter the real balance of social power in the countryside," as noted by Robert H. Dix in 1967, but merely to *distract* attention from leftist politics and pacify active state-antagonists in the countryside.[xix] Rural schools, consequently, lacked formal structure and good teacher qualifications. Additionally, the state blatantly "refused to establish education services past the primary level, a practice that remains largely present to this day."[xx]

Consequently, "throughout the 1960s and 1970s, 'only 10.8 percent of the [rural] population had had five years or more years of schooling' (Saunders et al, 1978: 100; Adams and Havens, 1966: 213)."[xxi] In failing to provide secondary or post-secondary education, those who did want to pursue a formal education were forced to leave the countryside en masse to the cities. Ironically, then, young people were forced to leave these very areas the JAC tried to "help."[xxii] This outright failure to extend the power of education to these rural communities was perhaps an attempt to prevent them from potentially increasing "the value and bargaining power" they could have if only they were sufficiently educated and mobilized, according to scholar David Kamens.[xxiii] As noted by Kamens, "Standards of cultural competence escalate as more of the population attains secondary and tertiary schooling."[xxiv] As people are better educated, they are better able to enter mainstream political life. With more education they come to understand the cultural assets for participation; "they are more issue oriented, better understand bureaucratic politics, know how to use the mass media, and are more able to recruit for and to fund electoral organizations. Hence, the expansion of education changes the aggregate distribution of political opportunities for participation."[xxv] In these rural communities, however, there was no hope to attend school beyond a couple of years. An educated and politicized rural mass was something the State, given their elitist and politically exclusive structure, would have wanted to avoid.

As a result, "'as time passed, *campesinos* became skeptical that much would come of Accion Comunal programs, and a majority came to view them cynically as proof that the government wanted to save money at their expense' (Henderson, 1958: 232)."[xxvi] Many JACs came to lose legitimacy. By the mid-1980s, some JACs started to engage in civic protests, seeking reformist measures to better satisfy the wants and needs of their communities. The State's response was to stop funding them and only support those that remained tied to their centralized state control. Inevitably, the social unrest did not quell. As it has been noted, "poorly performing procedural democracies could also be targets of regime overthrow; this is particular[ly] true if the bureaucratic elite is perceived to be out of touch or oppressive of mass constituencies (Fanon 1961)."[xxvii] Eventually, some JACs came to ally themselves against the State and with the FARC.[xxviii]

The Role of the FARC: Cultural Centers

Due to the state's inefficiency in meeting the demands of all of its people, especially in these rural regions, the FARC came to fill "the void by helping build roads and provide electricity, law enforcement, judges and other public services traditionally supplied by the state."[xxix] In turn, the FARC gained more support and mobilization. In an interview with one female respondent from Putumayo, it was explained: "The state has negated any forms of education in the countryside for decades and it is only through the FARC's schools that someone in the rural areas can have a chance of learning … […]… To many of us, the FARC are the government."[xxx]

So what kind of education do the FARC provide? To begin, their education facilities are referred to as "cultural centers." As described by James Brittain, they "are heavily used and resembled a jungle-like revolutionary museum; filled with pamphlets, books, music, and information related to Marxism, Colombia's political economy, and Latin American society," plastered with pictures of Marxist guerilla leader Che Guevara and past comandantes of the FARC. Attendees are males and females of various ethnicities and ages, including adults ranging from their 20s to their 50s. Younger students focus on elementary writing and numerical skills; more developed groups learn about advanced politics, economics, and history, along with topics such as imperialism, agrarian reform, political economy, wages, class structure, and hegemony.[xxxi]

However, while it is this promise of a complete education that often entices people to join, the education FARC members receive is only slightly fulfilled. Their education is one-sighted, mostly filled with socialist and FARC propaganda, of which they are obligated to read at least two hours daily. In fact, in an interview with former FARC members, they referred to it as "brainwashing or mind-control."[xxxii] These interviews conducted in July 2012 shed light onto how their education is skewed:

> While the FARC teaches traditional academic principles, these principles are also used by the group to buttress FARC concepts. For example, one of the interviewees - 'William' quoted from Sun Tzu's The Art of War, Machiavelli's The Prince, and Clausewitz's On War. He also quoted the economic theory of John Maynard Keynes. The FARC taught these concepts to him using incomplete data and texts to understand how the non-socialist world was wrong. Keynes' theories were used to show capitalism and how it was flawed, again using FARC rationale.[xxxiii]

Moreover, "any concepts outside of FARC accepted theories were considered irrational, false and could not be uttered."[xxxiv] Such pedagogy is one Paulo Freire would define as repressive: "The capability of banking education to minimize or annul the students' creative power and to stimulate their credulity serves the interests of the oppressors."[xxxv] In other words, the FARC does not educate members into being liberated, conscious persons, but rather indoctrinates them to retain dominion over them.

Brittain tries to justify the education system of the FARC, counteracting the argument that the FARC employs a "Stalinist method of manipulating intellectual endeavors."[xxxvi] He notes how in some cases the FARC have come to financially support combatants to attend universities throughout Colombia, a setting in which they would be open to other ideas. Van Dongen's article explains that FARC offers free tuition to lure the mostly poor University students into joining their recruitments.[xxxvii] Once students are recruited, they must then come to the FARC compounds and be trained and indoctrinated with their ideals. In short, a FARC education obviates thinking, inhibits creativity, and is something completely contrary to what Freire proposes. In his own words, "Those truly committed to the cause of liberation can accept neither the mechanistic concept of consciousness as an empty vessel to be filled, nor the use of banking methods of domination (propaganda, slogans—deposits) in the name of liberation."[xxxviii] The FARC's education system, consequently, fails in contributing to state-building — as it brainwashes its students to act violently against the State — and in forming democratic citizens — as is evident through its authoritative style of educating.

Analysis

As is evidenced right now, it seems that the education system in Rural Colombia has failed to promote any sense of democratic citizenship or participation. The State has apparently failed in providing adequate opportunities for education or ensuring the personal security of its citizens, factors that are "key to promoting greater citizen confidence in the institutions of representative democracy — and satisfaction with democracy in general."[xxxix] Their developmental attempts through JACs, for example, only contributed to delegitimizing their state presence. As explained by Bleck, "decades of poor state performance make many citizens question the utility of the state (Mbembe 1998)."[xl] As a consequence of the state's weakness, the FARC, as only one example, has come to fill the void. However, the FARC, in presenting itself as "compensating for state failure or neglect," has caused citizens to "develop additional and potentially competing attachments," namely with that of the FARC.[xli] Such an education thwarts any potential for positive allegiance to the State or forming democratic citizenship and participation. For the State, this *is* the "worse-case scenario" against which Bleck warned: "non-state schools could divide citizens, foster parochial attitudes, undermine state legitimacy, and remove one of, if not the only, sources of citizen contact with the state, thus decreasing political knowledge and participation."[xlii] Until the State stops waging war against these rural areas and starts implementing good, quality education services, rural communities will continue to see their welfare and survival as inextricably intertwined with that of the FARC.

However, due in part to its new 1991 Constitution of the Rights, the State has come to make some promising efforts to reform its education system. One example is the 1994 Ley General de Educacion (General Law of Education). This law demands that students be educated in 'justice, peace, democracy, solidarity...' (Art. 14, d) and in 'the social, ethical, moral and other values of human development' (Art. 20, f). Additionally, the Law establishes ethical education and human values (Art. 23, 4) as mandatory subjects in basic education.[xliii] To ensure citizenship competencies become an integral part of Colombia's formal education system, students take the Saber tests, which measure math, language, natural and social science and citizenship skills, at the end of Grade 5 (10-12 year olds) and Grade 9 (14-16-year-olds)."[xliv] Citizenship competence questions are also included in college entrance exams.[xlv] To guarantee nationwide acceptance and implementation of this Citizenship Competencies Program, the Ministry is now working with all the regional Secretariats of Education as well as other non-state actors. Such collaborative efforts between the State and non-state providers may have the double effect of not only increasing welfare provision but also "inducing greater citizens satisfaction with citizenship and potentially even leading to greater citizen compliance with the state and/or attachments to the national political community."[xlvi] While many challenges still remain, such as the difficulty in building these aforementioned alliances because of deep distrust of the government, the lack of accountability in overseeing this program, the need for the Ministry to better train educators in democratic ideals, and the need to avoid corruption in government contracts—which has delayed implementation across the country[xlvii] — this is a giant step forward in the State trying to develop informed and empowered, democratic citizens. Moreover, if the State works seriously on expanding educational opportunities for its rural constituents, such efforts, collaborated with this Citizenship Competencies Program, could have the potential to aid "democratic deepening and state-building in three important ways: 1) by empowering citizens and expanding their awareness of the democratic institutions around them; 2) by endowing students with the language of state bureaucracy, thus increasing their levels of internal efficacy; and 3) in the case of state schools, by building connections with parents through social service provision."[xlviii] All this could be possible, but the first key step is for the State to expand quality education services throughout all of Colombian territory, especially to its 25% living in rural areas.

Conclusion

Above all, the State of Colombia is making significant progress in trying to expand education access to all of its rural constituents. Vast improvements have been made from the early 1980s. At that time, coffee growers averaged only 3.4 years of schooling, but now the average is about 8 years, and while the total rural illiteracy rate is 19.5%, only 8.5% of rural 15- to 24-year-olds are illiterate."[xlix] Additionally, a promising advancement has been the Ministry's partnering with the Escuela Nueva (New School) program. Led by Vicky Colbert, Escuela Nueva "successfully combines participatory and student centered learning to achieve both short-term goals, such as improved academic achievements and self-esteem, and long-term goals like creating a more democratic and egalitarian society."[l] In fact, it's been noted that some schools in this program have outperformed urban schools in test scores.[li] This, along with the State's current ongoing peace negotiations with the FARC, are all steps towards one day creating a more unified nation, "a materially integrated society" characterized by the "relative moral, mental, and cultural unity of its inhabitants, who consciously suppose the state and its laws."[lii] If Colombia hopes to finally put an end to this six-decade long conflict, then the State must come to expand access to quality education institutions and sufficient opportunities to all of its constituents. With its willingness to collaborate with both domestic and international support, Colombia has the potential to implement an effective educational system that fosters genuine democratic citizenship and participation.

---

[i] Phil Price, "Waging Peace for Colombia's Youth: Countering the Attack on Education," *Human Rights and Human Welfare*, Topical Research Digest: Minority Rights (2010): 100.

[ii] Jaimie Bleck, *Democracy, Education, and Citizenship in Mali* (PhD diss., Cornell University Department of Government, 2011): 22-3.
[iii] Eric B. Ross, "Clearance as Development Strategy in Rural Colombia," *Peace Review: A Journal of Social Justice*, Vol. 19, No. 1 (8 March 2007): 59.
[iv] Mario Novelli, "Education, Conflict, and Social (In)justice: Insights from Colombia," *Educational Review*, Vol. 62, No. 3 (August 2010): 274.
[v] Frances Thomson, "The Agrarian Question and Violence in Colombia: Conflict and Development," *Journal of Agragarian Change*, Vol. 11, No. 3 (July 2011): 335.
[vi] Frances Thomson, "The Agrarian Question and Violence in Colombia: Conflict and Development," *Journal of Agragarian Change*, Vol. 11, No. 3 (July 2011): 328.
[vii] Patricia Grogg and Constanza Vieira, "Key Land Reform Accord in Colombia's Peace Talks," *Inter Press Service News Agency*, last modified May 27, 2013, http://www.ipsnews.net/2013/05/key-land-reform-accord-in-colombias-peace-talks/.
[viii] Frances Thomson, "The Agrarian Question and Violence in Colombia: Conflict and Development," *Journal of Agragarian Change*, Vol. 11, No. 3 (July 2011): 327.
[ix] International Fund for Agricultural Development (IFAD), "Rural poverty in Colombia," *Rural Poverty Portal*, 2011. accessed 5 Dec. 2013, http://www.ruralpovertyportal.org/country/home/tags/colombia.
[x] BBC News, "Colombia tops IDMC internally displaced people list," *Latin America and Caribbean*, last modified April 29, 2013, http://www.bbc.com/news/world-latin-america-22341119.
[xi] Library of Congress, "Colombia: A Country Study," *Federal Research Division*, last modified 2010, accessed December 8, 2013, xviii.
[xii] Educational Development Center, Inc., "Forum Unites Public Private, Private Actors Seeking to Improve Education in Colombia," *Education Development Center, Inc.: Learning transforms lives,* last modified 2011, accessed December 14, 2013.
[xiii] UNICEF, "Education Statistics: Colombia," *Division of Policy and Practice, Statistics and Monitoring Section*, last modified May 2008,

accessed December 5, 2013, http://www.unicef.org/infobycountry/colombia_statistics.html#117.

[xiv] Educational Development Center, Inc., "Forum Unites Public Private, Private Actors Seeking to Improve Education in Colombia," *Education Development Center, Inc.: Learning transforms lives,* last modified 2011, accessed December 14, 2013.

[xv] Educational Development Center, Inc., "Forum Unites Public Private, Private Actors Seeking to Improve Education in Colombia," *Education Development Center, Inc.: Learning transforms lives,* last modified 2011, accessed December 14, 2013.

[xvi] Library of Congress, "Colombia: A Country Study," *Federal Research Division*, last modified 2010, accessed December 8, 2013, 128.

[xvii] James J. Brittain, *Revolutionary Social Change in Colombia: The Origin and Direction of the FARC-EP* (New York: Pluto Press, 2010): 161.

[xviii] Amartya Sen, *Development as Freedom* (Westminster: Alfred A. Knopf Incorporation, 1999): 53.

[xix] James J. Brittain, *Revolutionary Social Change in Colombia: The Origin and Direction of the FARC-EP* (New York: Pluto Press, 2010): 161.

[xx] James J. Brittain, *Revolutionary Social Change in Colombia: The Origin and Direction of the FARC-EP* (New York: Pluto Press, 2010): 162.

[xxi] James J. Brittain, *Revolutionary Social Change in Colombia: The Origin and Direction of the FARC-EP* (New York: Pluto Press, 2010): 162.

[xxii] James J. Brittain, *Revolutionary Social Change in Colombia: The Origin and Direction of the FARC-EP* (New York: Pluto Press, 2010): 163.

[xxiii] David H. Kamens, "Education and Democracy: A Comparative Institutional Analysis," *Sociology of Education,* Vol 61, (April 1988): 120.

[xxiv] David H. Kamens, "Education and Democracy: A Comparative Institutional Analysis," *Sociology of Education,* Vol 61, (April 1988): 122.

[xxv] David H. Kamens, "Education and Democracy: A Comparative Institutional Analysis," *Sociology of Education,* Vol 61, (April 1988): 122.

[xxvi] James J. Brittain, *Revolutionary Social Change in Colombia: The*

Origin and Direction of the FARC-EP (New York: Pluto Press, 2010): 166.

xxvii Jaimie Bleck, *Democracy, Education, and Citizenship in Mali* (PhD diss., Cornell University Department of Government, 2011): 26.

xxviii James J. Brittain, *Revolutionary Social Change in Colombia: The Origin and Direction of the FARC-EP* (New York: Pluto Press, 2010): 166.

xxix James J. Brittain, *Revolutionary Social Change in Colombia: The Origin and Direction of the FARC-EP* (New York: Pluto Press, 2010): 102.

xxx James J. Brittain, *Revolutionary Social Change in Colombia: The Origin and Direction of the FARC-EP* (New York: Pluto Press, 2010): 106-7.

xxxi James J. Brittain, *Revolutionary Social Change in Colombia: The Origin and Direction of the FARC-EP* (New York: Pluto Press, 2010): 175.

xxxii Paul S. Nader, "Former Members' Perspectives are Key to Impacting the FARC," *Journal of Strategic Security*, Vol. 6, No. 1 (2013): 77.

xxxiii Paul S. Nader, "Former Members' Perspectives are Key to Impacting the FARC," *Journal of Strategic Security*, Vol. 6, No. 1 (2013): 76-7.

xxxiv Paul S. Nader, "Former Members' Perspectives are Key to Impacting the FARC," *Journal of Strategic Security*, Vol. 6, No. 1 (2013): 77.

xxxv Paulo Freire, *Pedagogy of the Oppressed* (New York: Continuum, 1968): 74.

xxxvi James J. Brittain, *Revolutionary Social Change in Colombia: The Origin and Direction of the FARC-EP* (New York: Pluto Press, 2010): 177.

xxxvii Rachel Van Dongen, "A coed's path from poli-sci major to leftist guerilla," *The Christian Science Monitor*, last modified February 10, 2004, accessed December 15, 2013, http://www.csmonitor.com/2004/0210/p01s02-woam.html.

xxxviii Paulo Freire, *Pedagogy of the Oppressed* (New York: Continuum, 1968): 79.

xxxix Scott Mainwaring, "The Crisis of Representation in the Andes,"

Journal of Democracy, Vol. 17, No. 3 (July 2006): 26.

[xl] Jaimie Bleck, *Democracy, Education, and Citizenship in Mali* (PhD diss., Cornell University Department of Government, 2011): 10.

[xli] Melani Claire Cammett and Lauren M. MacLean, "Introduction: the Political Consequences of Non-state Social Welfare in the Global South," *Studies in International Development*, Vol. 46, (2011): 15.

[xlii] Jaimie Bleck, *Democracy, Education, and Citizenship in Mali* (PhD diss., Cornell University Department of Government, 2011): 27.

[xliii] Rosario Jaramillo and Jose A. Mesa, "Citizenship Education as a Response to Colombia's Social and Political Context," *Journal of Moral Education*, Vol. 32, No. 4 (November 13, 2009): 469.

[xliv] Rosario Jaramillo and Jose A. Mesa, "Citizenship Education as a Response to Colombia's Social and Political Context," *Journal of Moral Education*, Vol. 32, No. 4 (November 13, 2009): 477.

[xlv] Rosario Jaramillo and Jose A. Mesa, "Citizenship Education as a Response to Colombia's Social and Political Context," *Journal of Moral Education*, Vol. 32, No. 4 (November 13, 2009): 478.

[xlvi] Melani Claire Cammett and Lauren M. MacLean, "Introduction: the Political Consequences of Non-state Social Welfare in the Global South," *Studies in International Development*, Vol. 46, (2011): 16.

[xlvii] Rosario Jaramillo and Jose A. Mesa, "Citizenship Education as a Response to Colombia's Social and Political Context," *Journal of Moral Education*, Vol. 32, No. 4 (November 13, 2009): 478, 482, 483.

[xlviii] Jaimie Bleck, *Democracy, Education, and Citizenship in Mali* (PhD diss., Cornell University Department of Government, 2011): 5.

[xlix] Educational Development Center, Inc., "Forum Unites Public Private, Private Actors Seeking to Improve Education in Colombia," *Education Development Center, Inc.: Learning transforms lives,* last modified 2011, accessed December 14, 2013.

[l] Phil Price, "Waging Peace for Colombia's Youth: Countering the Attack on Education," *Human Rights and Human Welfare*, Topical Research Digest: Minority Rights (2010): 101.

[li] Library of Congress, "Colombia: A Country Study," *Federal Research Division*, last modified 2010, accessed December 8, 2013, 129.

[lii] Eugene Weber, *Peasants into Frenchmen* (Stanford: Stanford University Press, 1975): 485.

Bibliography

Hernan Gutierrez, "Colombia: Overview of Corruption and Anti-Corruption," *Transperancy International,* last modified March 15, 2013, accessed November 23, 2013, http://www.transparency.org/whatwedo/answer/colombia_ove rview_of_corruption_and_anti_corruption.

The Economist, "Land reform in Colombia: Peace, land, and bread," *Americas,* last modified November 24, 2012, accessed December 5, 2013, http://www.economist.com/news/americas/21567087-hard-bargaining-starts-peace-land-and-bread.

Tariq Thachil, "Embedded Mobilization: Nonstate Service Provision as Electoral Strategy in India," *World Politics,* Vol. 63. No. 3, (July 2011): 432-356.

Protecting the Border;
China's Realist Motives behind Developing the West

Deanna Kolberg

Introduction

In China, nominally, "Open up the West" or the "Western Development Program" targeting Xinjiang, Tibet and other western provinces are policies meant to redress economic inequality between the rich East coast and impoverished West. In reality, the underlying goals of these policies were more complex. The development program was also meant to increase security by assimilating the minority groups in the region, protecting China's volatile border, and increasing the regional sphere of influence of the People's Republic of China (PRC) to its energy-rich western neighbors. Moving control beyond China's western border was and is crucial for the rising power in energy, trade, and regional stability. The ability to accomplish this comes from strong control of China's Western region, particularly the sparsely populated, heavily minority-concentrated areas of Xinjiang's border with Afghanistan, Kazakhstan, Kyrgyzstan, Tajikistan and Pakistan. By taking Xinjiang as a case study, I argue that this policy of "Western Development" was developed for security purposes, rather than simply economic reasons.

History

China has always had a security interest in the Western region. Since Xinjiang became a province during the Qing dynasty in 1884, the government has had a loose hold on the area. In the 1940s, the East Turkestan Republic formed with heavy backing by the USSR. In 1942, it transitioned to rule by the Kuomintang and then lost power to the PRC in 1949. The localization of China's power on the East coast left it increasingly vulnerable to attack by the Soviet Union, which had its eyes set on Xinjiang's natural resources, as well as to separatist forces within the country. Since the 1980s, Beijing has sought to secure control in the area of Xinjiang and Tibet through various development programs aimed at the western region of China. Particularly after the dissolution of Soviet states, the threat of separatism greatly increased in Xinjiang as ethnic Turkic people called for a unified Turkic state. After the violent Yining riots against Han Chinese in 1997, many Uighur people fled to Kazakhstan and Turkey, fearing state-led retribution.[i] Throughout the late 1990's, China's neighbors, including Afghanistan, allegedly provided training and border access to East Turkestan separatists.[ii]

In 1988, Zhao Ziyang introduced the "Coastal Economic Development Strategy" (沿海经 济发展战略), which focused primarily on developing the East coast and providing a basis for later development in the interior provinces.[iii] The non-coastal provinces at that time were frustrated with the country's trade structure. Coastal provinces added labor to raw goods from the interior provinces for export and "dumped" cheap goods produced for export on non-coastal provinces, competing with local businesses. This left the non-coastal provinces with no foreign cash reserves and little hope of building industry, increasing unrest in the region.[iv] In the late 1980s, Deng Xiaoping began promoting developing the interior to levels of "comparatively well off." According to Deng, the Eastern region had reached an adequate level of development to allow attention to be moved to the Western region. The official "Western Development Program" was started by Jiang Zemin at the Ninth National People's Congress in June of 1999.[v] To implement this policy, the government turned to the Xinjiang Production and Construction Corps (XPCC), currently a collection of 2.48 million state quasi-military workers. Before the fall of the Soviet Union, these laborers were meant to work on infrastructure projects, while also creating a first line of defense by populating and fortifying the border areas. Their role in border protection remained after the dissolution of the USSR as fears of separatism grew, and even today the XPCC is able to perform this dual role. In an interview with BBC in 2005, a soldier-turned-farmer XPCC member described his duty as "(primarily) to defend the land and protect the border. Growing crops, the economy — that's a number two.'"[vi] Through transplanting a large population of loyal Han Chinese, the Chinese Communist Party's (CCP) hoped to create official and unofficial border protection. Due in large part to this program, the Han population in Xinjiang tripled in the ten years following the program's start in 1990.

The Role of Sinicization in Quelling Separatism

Although mass migration has the potential to back-fire in the short-term, the central government sees an increase in Han Chinese and the growth of their influence in the region, or the sinicization, of Xinjiang as a way to promote national unity and, more importantly, long-term stability.[vii] By forging connections between the Han and ethnic minorities, Beijing hopes the Turkic people of Xinjiang will see more in common with their fellow Chinese citizen rather than ethnic and culturally similar Muslims on the other side of the border. Throughout the course of the Western Development policy, the population of Uighurs has decreased to around 30-40%, less than half the percentage it once was.[viii] As made evident by local unrest, this policy increased fears among minority groups of losing their unique culture, and more so, increased anti-Han sentiment when Han Chinese were given job preference in state industries and increasingly Han-controlled non-government sectors.[ix]

Increasing the Han population in Xinjiang was meant to work in conjunction with economic development to quell anti-nationalist sentiment among ethnic minorities. A primary aim of the Western Development program was to increase economic viability in the region, which was blatantly observed by policymakers as a method to quell separatism. As one official noted:

> "The aim of the government's program to develop China's western provinces is to prevent China's foreign enemies using poverty to create a Kosovo-style crisis in the region ... Providing ethnic minorities in those regions with more economic development would help guarantee the inviolability of China's borders and political and social stability in the region."[x]

Rhetoric such as this demonstrates the CCP's cognizance of the connection between an individual's income and national security. Income disparity between both the East and West and urban and rural Xinjiang remains high, suggesting that economic development is a secondary goal and only pursued when part of a larger goal of maintaining stability.[xi]

Infrastructure and Resource Extraction

To increase economic development, a major component of the tenth and eleventh five-year plans was to fund large infrastructure projects in rail, water and oil pipelines.[xii] Since the inception of the 2000 Western Development program, rail lines have been added to better connect the West with the East, and the West with Kazakhstan and other Central Asian countries. A high-speed rail from Lanzhou to Urumqi is currently under construction.[xiii] The central government funded these improvements to create a positive investment environment for encouraging foreign direct investment (FDI) in the area.

Infrastructure not only assists in economic development of the region, but facilitates more efficient transfer of natural resources to the dry, energy-thirsty East coast. In 2000, Xinjiang was estimated to have 52.5% of the country's water, 58% of natural gas reserves, and over half of the country's mineral reserves.[xiv] China's reliance on these key natural resources is unmistakable, and is a serious security threat to the PRC. Diversifying and controlling energy supplies is crucial to China in light of the Arab Spring and the South China Sea disputes to ensure the continuous fuelling of production.[xv]

Despite large investment in other areas, Xinjiang's economy remains focused on resource extraction. Bequelin, a scholar of Xinjiang's economic development geopolitical strategy, writes;

"It's foreign trade structure reflects that Xinjiang is basically a transit point... a large proportion is actually politically motivated barter-trade between China and it's central Asian neighbors (Kazakhstan accounts for half of the volume) and Xinjiang's "exports" are essentially manufactured goods produced in the coastal areas."[xvi]

He highlights that an essential component of this trade relationship is the neighboring countries. The construction of rail lines from Gansu to Xinjiang and onward to places like Kazakhstan and Uzbekistan facilitates such a relationship, but the true economic effects are felt more in the East where these goods are produced.[xvii]

Anti-terrorism and Influence

Xinjiang's connection to Central Asian states through the Eurasian Land Bridge is increasingly important in security and international trade. In the aftermath of September 11th, 2001, the central government sent an additional 40,000 troops to Xinjiang's border to defend against increased instability in Central Asia. This instability had potential to instigate separatist terrorism activities in China through connections with Osama bin Laden.[xviii] If Beijing truly is concerned about terrorism flowing from across the border, then the absence of U.S. troop involvement in Afghanistan means the PRC may need to increase its presence to fight terrorist forces along its border.

The drawdown of U.S. troops in Afghanistan leaves a power vacuum in the region, giving China the opportunity and the impetus to extend its sphere of influence into the resource-heavy countries and crucial transportation networks of Central Asia. Reviving Silk Road trade routes and extending connections not only facilitates the easy transport of resource imports and manufactured exports, but also ensures that countries throughout the region are increasingly reliant on China for economic support, rather than the United States and Russia. This, in turn, gives China higher international credibility and undeniable influence reaching as far as Europe's periphery. In addition, China has a range of assets in the country, ranging from direct investment to Chinese-backed projects. One mine in Aynak (an area with strong Haqqani Network presence), backed by the state-owned Metallurgical Company of China, is worth almost $3.5 billion. As an act of diplomacy, Beijing offered the Afghan government 200 million yuan in grants last year. Only sharing a small border with China, Beijing is also looking towards other Central Asian countries to diversify its international investments as the costs of securing assets in Afghanistan increase.[xix]

Furthermore, "South-South Trade" is a prime driver of policy between China and its Western neighbors, resulting in multiple conferences and the creation of the Shanghai Cooperation Organization (SCO), made up of Russia, Tajikistan, Kyrgyzstan, Kazakhstan, Uzbekistan, and, of course, China.[xx] In addition to providing an area for dialogue on trade agreements, the SCO has a specific committee for preventing terrorism, separatism, and extremism called the Executive Committee of Regional Counter-terrorism Structure.[xxi] By establishing this body, China has made it clear that it will not be providing the institutions for trade agreements without receiving security benefits in return.

Conclusion

Undoubtedly, Xinjiang plays a strong role in China's geopolitical and economic strategy. From sinicization strategies to resource-extracting infrastructure, evidence repeatedly asserts that Beijing's prime concern in the "development" of the region has an overwhelmingly realist tone. China has extended large amounts of investment in infrastructure development to the Western regions, not only to reduce the poverty experienced by many millions of minorities, but also to protect sovereignty from Xi'an to China's far western border and to increase China's sphere of influence throughout Central Asia. By looking at Xinjiang as an example, we can see more complex reasoning than simple economic motivations. Developing Xinjiang brings immense national security benefits to the People's Republic of China.

i Lai Hongyi, "China's Western Development Program: Its Rationale, Implementation, and Prospects," *Modern China 28.4* (October 2002): 432-46.

ii Lai Hongyi, "China's Western Development Program: Its Rationale, Implementation, and Prospects," *Modern China 28.4* (October 2002): 432-46.

iii Lai Hongyi, "China's Western Development Program: Its Rationale, Implementation, and Prospects," *Modern China 28.4* (October 2002): 432-46.

iv Xu Bingwen, Zhou Shushi, Li Xiaofan, and Li Hehu, "中国西北地区经济发展战略改论," (An introduction to the strategy of economic development in China's northwestern region), *Jingji guanli chubans*, Beijing (1992).

v Lai Hongyi, "China's Western Development Program: Its Rationale, Implementation, and Prospects," *Modern China 28.4* (October 2002): 432-46.

vi Quentin Sommerville, "China's Western Border 'Defenders,'" *BBC News*, last modified November 17, 2005, accessed March 6, 2013, http://news.bbc.co.uk/2/hi/asia-pacific/4445736.stm.

vii Nicholas Bequelin, "Staged Development in Xinjiang," *The China Quarterly 178* (2004): 358-378.

viii Ting Xu, "High Stakes for China in Xinjiang," Real Clear World, last modified 2012, accessed March 6, 2013, http://www.realclearworld.com/articles/2012/12/13/high_stakes_for_c hina_in_xinjiang_100405.html.

ix Zang Xiaowei, "Affirmative Action, Economic Reforms, and Han-Uyghur Variation in Job Attainment in the State Sector in Urumqi," *The China Quarterly 202* (2010): 344-361.

x Matthew D. Moneyhon, "China's great western development project in Xinjiang: economic palliative, or political trojan horse?" *Denver Journal of International Law and Policy 31.3* (2003): 491+.

xi Zhu, Yuchao & Dongyan Blachford, "Economic Expansion, Marketization, and Their Social Impact on China's Ethnic Minorities in Xinjiang and Tibet," *Asian Survey 52* (2012): 714-733.

xii Xinhua News Agency, "Five-Year Guidelines Set for Western Development," last modified December 9, 2006, http://www.china.org.cn/english/GS-e/191781.htm.

[xiii] The Economist, "Faster than a Speeding Bullet," *China,* November 9, 2013.

[xiv] Lai Hongyi, "China's Western Development Program: Its Rationale, Implementation, and Prospects," *Modern China 28.4* (October 2002): 432-46.

[xv] Ting Xu, "High Stakes for China in Xinjiang," Real Clear World, last modified 2012, accessed March 6, 2013, http://www.realclearworld.com/articles/2012/12/13/high_stakes_for_c hina_in_xinjiang_100405.html.

[xvi] Nicholas Bequelin, "Staged Dev. in Xinjiang," *The China Quarterly 178* (2004): 358-372.

[xvii] Nicholas Bequelin, "Staged Dev. in Xinjiang," *The China Quarterly 178* (2004): 358-378.

[xviii] Matthew D. Moneyhon, "China's great western development project in Xinjiang: economic palliative, or political trojan horse?" *Denver Journal of International Law and Policy 31.3* (2003): 491+.

[xix] Teddy Ng, "China's Dilemma in Afghanistan," South China Morning Post, accessed December 5, 2013, http://www.scmp.com/news/china/article/1373109/chinas-dilemma-afghanistan.

[xx] Xinhua News Agency, "Five-Year Guidelines Set for Western Development," last modified December 9, 2006, http://www.china.org.cn/english/GS-e/191781.htm.

[xxi] The Shanghai Cooperation Organization, *The Executive Committee of the Regional Counter-Terrorism Structure*, accessed March 7, 2013, http://www.sectsco.org/EN123/AntiTerrorism.asp.

The Effect of Minimum Wages on Happiness

Jenna Nizamoff

Talks of raising the national minimum wage have begun resurfacing in America. Proponents of a minimum wage increase from $7.25 to $10.10, including President Barack Obama, believe that the minimum wage has not kept up with inflation and does not allow Americans to meet the current costs of living, citing that a full-time worker making the minimum wage only brings in about $15,000 a year in income[i], which is only slightly above the national poverty line of $11,490 for a one-person household. McDonald's workers are protesting across the country for higher wages with signs proclaiming, "We can't survive on $7.25!"[ii] Empirically, these disgruntled workers may be right: over 52 percent of families whose earners work in the fast food industry rely on public assistance programs such as food stamps and welfare to make ends meet, which costs taxpayers about $7 billion per year.[iii]

Those in favor of market solutions, and therefore against minimum wages, have a counterargument. They believe that an increase in the minimum wage will hurt low-wage workers more than it will help. Traditional economic theory states that a minimum wage above the marginal product of labor will lead to increased unemployment. It shows that if employers must pay workers more money than they are worth, they will hire fewer workers to offset the increased costs. Therefore, although a higher minimum wage could allow some workers to pay their bills, it would throw others into deeper poverty by causing them to lose their jobs.

This paper aims to look at a different but related question, namely, whether or not a minimum wage makes a population happier. Since people would arguably be happier if they could make enough money to cover their costs of living and less happy if the unemployment rate rose, the answer to such a question could help determine which effect is the dominant force and if an overall increase in the minimum wage is a good policy for society. Although scant research has been done on a minimum wage's effect on happiness, one could assume that research done on the size of the positive and negative effects of minimum wages could indicate whether or not it would leave a population happier. Therefore, I begin by reviewing relevant economic theory and research on the effects of a minimum wage increase to provide background information and describe what related questions have been approached and answered. I then describe the data and method used to answer this question, followed by the interpretation of such results as well as the implications.

Minimum Wage Theory and Empirical Research

The real effect of a minimum wage is one of the most debated topics in economics. As the Center for Economic and Policy Research (CEPR) states, "the standard competitive model makes stark predictions about the employment effects of the minimum wage: a binding minimum wage will price at least some low-wage workers out of jobs and will unambiguously lower employment."[iv] In other words, if the price of labor rises, employers will demand fewer workers. This creates an inefficiency in the labor market, leaving some people better off, e.g., with higher wages and thus able to meet their costs of living, and others without a job and thus less able to meet their costs of living.

Although a minimum wage theoretically leads to inefficiencies in the market, namely, demand for labor does not meet labor supply, proponents of the move suggest that it does less harm than good. A report done by the International Labor Organization (ILO) asserts that "minimum wages can be a powerful tool for supporting decent work goals and can be a crucial complement to the strengthening of social protection floors and poverty alleviation efforts."[v] In other words, minimum wages do not result in only negative effects because a well-designed policy can help reduce inequality and eliminate poverty within a society. The ILO cites four cases in which minimum wage policies have benefitted society: in Brazil, the minimum wage policy is "one of the most widely credited measures to explain the reduction in poverty"; in China, "coordinated minimum wage increases…have been a key part of a strategy to reduce inequality"; in the United Kingdom, where minimum wages were eliminated then reintroduced, "political experts have identified the minimum wage as a successful policy"; and in the United States, a higher minimum wage has "reduced poverty and inequality and provided a stimulus to the economy."[vi]

Besides social benefits, the ILO and other minimum wage proponents believe minimum wage policies can help increase demand for consumables, citing that "the redistributive effect of minimum wages towards low-paid workers with a high propensity to consume" leads to more consumption than would occur if employers and high-earners kept the extra money they lose through redistribution. This positive economic effect could help stimulate economies through increased consumption, leading to higher firm profits, which would allow them the ability to retain employees instead of firing some due to an increased minimum wage.

In the end, economic theory is divided when it comes to minimum wage; there is no conclusive "yes" or "no" to whether or not it is beneficial. Therefore, we must look to empirical evidence. Multiple studies have been conducted to test the effects of increasing the minimum wage on employment and many have contradicted each other; for example, recent studies tend to show that an increase in the minimum wage does not have significant effects on employment while older studies show that it does. Thankfully, the Center for Economic and Policy Research compiled a convenient meta-report that pulls together the findings from all the studies on minimum wage effects on employment since 2000. They note that, as stated previously, most findings show that minimum wage has no or a negligible effect on employment. The CEPR then looks into why the empirical evidence contradicts conventional economic theory.

The group introduces three different theoretical approaches to the minimum wage that allow for adjustment channels, "through which cost increases associated with the minimum wage change... the behavior of firms, with impacts on workers, consumers, owners and other agents."[vii] These three theories include the competitive model, which "implies that binding minimum wages will reduce employment"; the institutional model, which "allows for several additional channels of adjustment to a minimum wage increase... most importantly an increase in productivity"; and the dynamic monopsony model, which allows for the possibility that "the minimum wage reduces the costs of turnover to low-wage employers."[viii] The possible channels through which the effects of an increase in the minimum wage could be adjusted are: a reduction in hours worked, a reduction in non-wage benefits, a reduction in training, changes in employment composition, higher prices for consumers, improvements in efficiency, efficiency wage responses from workers, wage compression (lowering the wages for the top earners), reduction in firm profits, increases in demand caused by the stimulus of a minimum wage, and reduced worker turnover.[ix]

After testing for significant changes in the adjustment channels after minimum wage hikes, the CEPR found that the only channels that experienced statistically significant changes proved to be reductions in labor turnover, improvements in organizational efficiency, small prices increases and reductions in wages of higher earners.[x] These findings imply that, overall, an increase in the minimum wage does not seem to negatively impact workers. Only one of the channels that was significantly adjusted after a minimum wage hike impacted worker salaries; none impacted employment or hours. Therefore, from the relevant literature one can assume that workers only benefit from an increase in the minimum wage; thus, we can theorize that a minimum wage hike increases a country's happiness.

Data and Methods

The data source for this study is twofold; the life satisfaction, or happiness, levels come from the World Value Survey and the minimum wage data comes from the Organization for Economic Cooperation and Development (OECD). The sample used was OECD countries; for the purposes of the study, limiting the sample to developed countries seemed the most plausible way to control for unknown variables that could affect levels of happiness. The minimum wage data is from the year 2012 and compares the minimum wage levels across countries by listing wages in purchasing power parity in terms of US dollars.

Of the thirty-four OECD members, eight do not have national minimum wages. These countries include: Denmark, Finland, Germany, Iceland, Italy, Norway, Sweden and Switzerland. Of these eight countries, wages in Demark, Finland, Germany, Iceland, Italy, Norway, and Switzerland are determined by binding collective bargaining agreements, usually applicable for different sectors of the economy.[xi] In Sweden, wages are determined "by taking into account the responsibility and level of difficulty of the work tasks and the worker performance of these tasks… as well as the work environment, conditions and market forces," according to the International Labor Organization.[xii]

To compare happiness across countries, this study completed two different regressions. One measured the effect of having a minimum wage on happiness; in this test, all thirty-four OECD members were used. The other regression only looked at countries that have a legislated minimum wage and sought to find the relationship between the size of the minimum wage and happiness.

Happiness as measured by the World Values Survey serves as the dependent variable in this analysis. The variables used for the first regression, or the one testing the effect of whether or not a country has a minimum wage on happiness, include a dummy variable for minimum wage; income satisfaction; the level of trust participants have; sex; age; age squared to account for errors; whether or not participants are married; whether or not the chief earner of the household is unemployed; income level; and church attendance. The variables used for the second regression are similar; the only difference is that the level of the minimum wage replaces the dummy variable for minimum wage. The variables for whether or not participants are married and whether or not the chief earner of the house is unemployed are dummy variables, as well.

The models tests against the null hypotheses that 1) whether or not a country has a minimum wage does not affect happiness, and 2) the level of a country's minimum wage does not affect happiness. The results for the first regression, which tests the relationship between whether or not a country has a minimum wage and happiness, are listed below:

Table One: Effect of having a minimum wage on happiness	
Variable	Coefficient
Minimum Wage (Dummy)	-.3766904** .1385166

Income Satisfaction	.3594413*** .0027978
Trust	-.2292485*** .0132773
Sex	-.0457403*** .0123645
Age	-.0312047*** .0022186
Agesq	.0002625*** .0000232
Married (Dummy)	.4278105*** .0144354
Chief Earner Unemployed (Dummy)	-.3711347*** .0390866
Income	-.0035594 .0027838
Church Attendance	-.0366065*** .0026666
Significance: (*) .1 (**) .05 (***) .01	

The results for the second regression, which test whether or not the level of a minimum wage affects happiness, are listed below:

Table Two: Effect of the minimum wage level on happiness	
Variable	**Coefficient**
Minimum Wage	.0536617* .0274796
Income Satisfaction	.3748039*** .0032669

Trust	-.1856774*** .0157673
Sex	-.0535228*** .0145119
Age	-.0287808*** -.0025929
Agesq	.000253*** .0000272
Married (Dummy)	.4177337*** .0169109
Chief Earner Unemployed (Dummy)	-.3141576*** .0448418
Income	.0008787 .0033026
Church Attendance	-.0343729*** .0030303
Significance: (*) .1 (**) .05 (***) .01	

Analysis of Results

The tables above show some interesting, unexpected results. Table One shows that all variables are significant besides level of income. Whether or not a country has a minimum wage is significant at the .05 level; however, the coefficient is negative, implying that a country is less happy if it has a legislated minimum wage. This is not what we would expect from the literature, which implies that a minimum wage has virtually no real negative effects on a population, especially workers.

The results are especially peculiar when compared to Table Two, which shows a positive, significant effect of minimum wage level on happiness; that is, the higher the level of a minimum wage, the happier a population is. Based off of the results of Table One, an observer of the data would think there was something wrong with the regression.

Although such results seem strange, they actually make sense. The regression results outlined in Table One include all thirty-four

OECD countries, including the seven that participate in collective bargaining to determine wages instead of using a legislated minimum wage. Those seven countries, all of which are notoriously happy, could be throwing off the regression line, even to a point in which it appears negative. Below is a graph that plots each country's happiness level versus minimum wage:

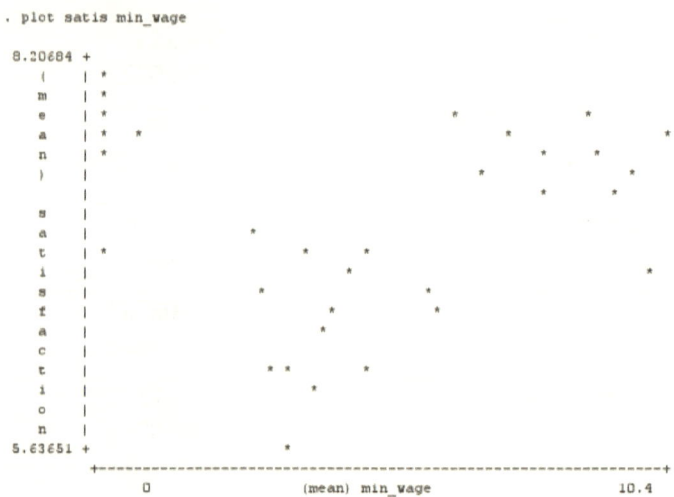

One can see from the plot above that, when the countries without a minimum wage are removed, a positive, upward-sloping relationship exists between minimum wage level and happiness. The results in Table One are thrown off by the high levels of happiness seen in countries without a legislated minimum wage. Therefore, among countries that do have a national, legislated minimum wage, there is a statistically significant relationship showing that a higher wage level makes a population happier.

If there is a positive relationship between minimum wage level and happiness, why do countries without a minimum wage report such high levels of happiness? One explanation could be that these countries are happier due to other reasons unrelated to the minimum wage; however, variables used in the regression should control for such errors, so the results should be due to other explanations. The most plausible reason for the high levels of reported happiness is that workers achieve better results through collective bargaining agreements; that is, workers whose wages are determined through collective bargaining are more satisfied with the results than those whose wages are determined by national legislation. This could imply that workers benefit more not from a minimum wage, but from a collective bargaining unit such as a labor organization negotiating for their wages. Although this seems to garner the best results for laborers, if a country has a legislated minimum wage, its general population will report greater satisfaction with higher wage levels.

Implications and Conclusion

Using minimum wage data from the OECD and life satisfaction data from the World Values Survey, this study attempted to measure the effect of a minimum wage on happiness. The results show that, among countries with a legislated minimum wage, such as the United States, people are happier with higher minimum wages. Among all OECD countries there is a statistically significant, negative relationship between minimum wages and happiness; that is, having a minimum wage makes countries less happy. However, this could simply indicate that countries which use collective bargaining through representative groups, such as labor unions, to determine minimum wages have better outcomes; that is, workers may get paid higher wages or be more satisfied due to other aspects of collective bargaining groups, such as a feeling of solidarity or job security.

Further work should be done to determine why countries without a national, legislated minimum wage report more happiness. Do they achieve higher incomes through collective bargaining? Do they feel solidarity as part of a labor organization, and thus feel more life satisfaction? Looking into questions such as these could determine how to enhance the lives of citizens, even if it means doing away with legislated minimum wages in exchange for more effective methods of wage setting.

This study has implications extending to the current debate over whether or not to raise the minimum wage in America from $7.25 to $10.10, as well as for countries around the world. Because relevant literature testing the effects of minimum wage increases found no significant negative effects on employment, coupled with the fact that higher minimum wages make a population happier, a well-designed minimum wage package could benefit society tremendously. If raised too high it could have deleterious effects on employment, but a wage that helps employees pay their costs of living could enhance their life satisfaction as well as take a burden off of taxpayers, who currently support many minimum-wage earners through additional help, such as food stamps and welfare.

ⁱ Berfield, Susan. "Fast-Food Wages Come With a $7 Billion Side of Public Assistance." *Bloomberg Businessweek*. 15 Oct 2013: n. page. Web. 18 Dec. 2013.

ⁱⁱ Jargon, Julie. "McDonald's Staffer: Full-Time and at the Food Bank?." *Wall Street Journal*. 24 Oct 2013: n. page. Web. 18 Dec. 2013.

ⁱⁱⁱ Berfield, *Fast-Food Wages*.

^{iv} Schmitt, John. "Why Does the Minimum Wage Have No Discernible Effect on Employment?." . Center for Economic and Policy Research, n.d. Web. 18 Dec 2013., 11.

^v "World of Work Report 2013: Repairing the Economic and Social Fabric." *International Labor Organization*. 2013: Web. 18 Dec. 2013.

^{vi} International Labor Organization. *World of Work Report 2013*.

^{vii} Schmitt, *Why Does the Minimum Wage*, 11.

^{viii} Schmitt, *Why Does the Minimum Wage*, 12-13.

^{ix} Schmitt, *Why Does the Minimum Wage*, 15-21.

^x Schmitt, *Why Does the Minimum Wage*, 22.

^{xi} "Conditions of Work and Employment Programme."*International Labor Organization* (2012): *Conditions oj Work and Employment (TRAVAIL)*. Web. 18 Dec 2013.

^{xii} International Labor Organization. *Conditions of Work and Employment Programme.*

A Tale of Two Swing States: Colorado and North Carolina

Zoe Rae Rote

In 2008, San Miguel County in southwestern Colorado cast 76.99% of its votes for Democratic candidate Barack Obama.[i] My sparsely populated county of 4,350 voters was the most Democratic county in the state; Telluride, my hometown, was the liberal hub of that county. Geographically isolated and surrounded by homogeneous political views, I always assumed that these liberal ideologies were the norm. Leading up to the 2008 presidential election, I was convinced that Obama would win my "swing state" because it seemed like *everyone* was a Democrat. That assumption was sharply challenged when I moved to Greensboro, North Carolina in August of 2008. I witnessed the polarity of American politics for the first time, and my new peers were shocked when Obama beat McCain by a razor-thin margin in 2008. Four years later, Colorado and North Carolina received political attention again as sought-after swing states. While Obama managed to capture Colorado for the second election in a row, North Carolina became the only swing state that Obama lost in 2012. This paper will explore why Obama won Colorado in both 2008 and 2012 but won North Carolina only in 2008. I have concluded that Colorado is on an upward Democratic trajectory because of demographic changes, while North Carolina's 2008 results were an anomaly in a state of political transition.

From 1968 to 2008, Colorado and North Carolina consistently voted Republican in presidential elections. Each state had only one exception during that fifty-year span; Colorado voted for Clinton in 1992 and North Carolina supported Carter in 1976.[ii] Because both states were reliably Republican for half a century, the fact that Obama won both Colorado and North Carolina in 2008 was a jolt to the Republican Party. In Colorado, Obama beat McCain by a large margin of 8.95 percentage points. He won 53.66% of the votes while McCain captured 44.71%. Although Obama's margin of victory shrunk to 5.36 points in 2012, he still won a decisive victory with 51.45% of the vote over Romney's 46.09%.[iii] Because Colorado's outcome remained constant in both elections, I chose to analyze this state first. In order to provide a foundation for my analysis, I will first explain why Colorado voted democratically in 2008 and then discuss how Obama was able to repeat his victory in 2012.

In my investigation into Census data and voter records revealed that Colorado voted Democrat in 2008 because of demographic changes, particularly in Hispanic[iv] and urban populations. In 2004, when Bush won 51.69% of the vote in Colorado,[v] Latinos made up 8% of voters in the state's presidential election. By 2008, that figure had risen to 13%.[vi] Hence, the number of Latinos in Colorado who voted in the presidential election jumped from approximately 170,426 voters in 2004 to 312,191 voters in 2008.[vii] An increase in 141,765 Latino voters in one four-year cycle is monumental, particularly because Kerry lost to Bush by a smaller margin in 2004.[viii]

Much of Kerry's support in Colorado came from the Hispanic population. According to CNN exit polls, Kerry won seven percent more of the Latino vote in 2004 than Obama won in 2008.[ix] At first, it seems like this data contradicts the hypothesis that the increasing Latino population facilitated Obama's victory in 2008. However, although the percentage of Hispanic support for the Democratic candidate decreased from 68% to 61%,[x] the actual number of Latino votes cast for the Democratic candidate rose substantially. Kerry won 68% of 170,426 Latino votes, which yielded approximately 115,890 votes for the Democratic candidate. In 2008, on the other hand, Obama won approximately 190,437 Latino votes.[xi] Although the margin of victory decreased by seven points, the net increase in the number of Latino votes compensated for this decrease in the percentage of Latino support.

The same trend continued in 2012 more convincingly than before. In 2012, Latinos comprised 14% of Colorado's voters and cast 75% of their votes for Obama. This means that Obama won approximately 270,044 Latino votes, an increase of nearly 80,000 Democratic votes from the previous election.[xii] This data support the hypothesis that Obama's back-to-back wins represent a trend instead of an erratic hiccup in Colorado politics, because the growth in the percentage of Latino voters is indicative of rapid growth in the Latino population throughout the state. This trend will continue if Democratic candidates continue to win large majorities of the

Hispanic vote. According to the U.S. Census Bureau, Hispanics comprised 17.1% of Colorado's population in 2000. By 2010, Hispanics made up 20.7% of the state's population and their numbers had broken one million.[xiii] If this growth continues, Latinos will have an amplified impact on state politics because of their increased voting power.

Moreover, the Census underestimates the number of Latinos living in Colorado because the government has difficulty estimating the number of undocumented immigrants. Many undocumented immigrants are fearful of responding to the Census because they fear deportation or other negative consequences. Therefore, the Census underestimates the widespread influence of Latinos. This further supports the conclusion that Latinos in Colorado will play a large role in state politics for years to come because more supporters and potential supporters exist than the Census accounts for. As long as the Democratic Party continues to appeal to Latinos, the trend of Democratic strength will accompany the growth in the Hispanic population.

Since 2000, Colorado has experienced not only increasing Latino populations but also a population influx into urban areas. This is important because urban population growth corresponds with the rising strength of the Democratic Party in Colorado. There is a strong nationwide correlation between urban centers and Democratic voting, and Obama managed to win back-to-back elections in Colorado as the state's population centers grew steadily. Between 2000 and 2012, Colorado experienced a 17% increase in population, totaling 5,187,582 residents in 2012.[xiv] Knowing which counties these people moved into enables us to determine whether Democrats or Republicans are moving into the state and where they are settling down. Analyzing Colorado's seven most populous counties will be the starting point of this approach.

Of these seven counties, only the largest voted Republican in 2008 and 2012. This Republican outlier, El Paso County, experienced a 19.6% growth rate between 2000 and 2012.[xv] In comparison, the remaining six most populous counties all voted for Obama with at least a 9-point margin in 2008 and at least a 4.85-point margin in 2012.[xvi] Three of these six counties also had population growth rates larger than Colorado's growth rate; Arapahoe County grew by 17.5%,

Laramer County grew by 18.5%, and Adams County grew by 23.5%.[xvii] Combined, these three counties alone contain more than double the population of El Paso County. Although the largest county in Colorado consistently votes Republican, this does not indicate which candidate the entire state will support because the six other most populous counties overshadow El Paso County. These expanding Democratic population centers indicate that Democrats are moving into the state and settling in urban areas. This trend supports the hypothesis that demographic change, particularly for Hispanics and urban centers, explains Barack Obama's victories in Colorado.

As I analyzed Census data and voter registration records for Colorado, the trend of demographic change leading to higher Democratic support became clear. The same eureka moment did not occur as I studied North Carolina, however. North Carolina is an anomaly because much of the data I found indicates that the state should have repeated its 2008 outcome in 2012. This did not happen. In 2008, Obama won 49.7% of the popular vote, only 0.32 points ahead of McCain's 49.38%.[xviii] A mere 14,177 votes enabled Obama to capture the state's 15 electoral votes. It was an incredibly close election. Four years later, Romney took back North Carolina with 50.39% of the vote, leading Obama's 48.35% by 2.04 points.[xix] In an attempt to answer why Obama won North Carolina in 2008 but failed to capture it again in 2012, I examined various factors that all failed to explain this phenomenon. The inconclusiveness of the data and the razor-thin margin with which Obama won in 2008 lead me to speculate that Obama's victory was an anomaly. Unlike the trend in Colorado, a likeable candidate and North Carolina's position of political flux explain these results.

As I tried to understand North Carolina's recent voting outcomes, I first analyzed the state's data on registered voters for 2008 and 2012. If the proportion of registered Republicans was much higher than that of Democrats in 2012, this would indicate an influx of non-native Republicans or converted Democrats into the state. The data disproved this theory, however. According to the North Carolina State Board of Elections, the number of registered Republicans increased by 2.6% between 2008 and 2012, compared to a 6.1% increase of registered voters overall.[xx] Unaffiliated voters experienced the largest increase overall, both proportionally and in raw numbers.

This data indicates that the small increase in Republican registered voters does not account for the state's support of Romney in 2012. A different factor or combination of factors must be responsible for the change.

During this search, it became obvious that registered voter identification is a poor indicator of states' election outcomes. In Colorado, there were more registered Republicans than Democrats in both 2008 and 2012, even though Obama won both of these elections. The registered voter records are even more misleading in North Carolina. In 2012, when Romney won North Carolina by 92,004 votes, there were 810,861 *more* registered Democrats than registered Republicans in the state.[xxi] In addition, in both 2008 and 2012, the Republican candidate won more votes than the total number of registered Republican voters in North Carolina.[xxii] It became quite clear that registered voter identification is not an accurate indication of voting results, more so in North Carolina than in Colorado. Earl and Merle Black's theory that party identification records "*exaggerate* Democratic strength and *underestimate* Republican strength" in Southern states supports this discovery.[xxiii]

Before exploring Black and Black's theory, it is important to understand North Carolina's political history because this theory applies to states from the Old South with deep Democratic roots. From 1876 to 1964, North Carolina voted Democrat in all but one election.[xxiv] In contrast to today's reliably Republican South, the Old South was staunchly Democratic from post-Reconstruction until the latter half of the twentieth century. Instead of relying only on voter registration data, Black and Black analyze both partisanship and ideology. In doing so, they find that Democratic strength is exaggerated by party identification because "conservative Democrats have not dependably supported Democratic presidential candidates."[xxv] On the other hand, conservative, moderate, and liberal Republicans dependably vote for the Republican candidate, as do conservative independents. This broadly explains why Democrats are overrepresented by party identification.

In addition, older North Carolinians may have registered as Democrats before the "great white shift" in the state's voting patterns. Instead of going through the hassle of changing their party identification, these voters have simply changed the way they vote.

Alternatively, old-timers may be unable to bring themselves to register as Republicans because of their deep connection to the Old Democratic South. Nonetheless, they will vote for the conservative candidate they support, most often a Republican. This supports the hypothesis that party identification is an inaccurate determinant of political equilibrium in the Old South. Colorado, on the other hand, does not comply as strongly with this theory because it never belonged to a regional, conservative voting bloc. The Old South's political history is the bedrock of this theory.

After determining that changes in voter registration could not explain North Carolina's anomaly, I next looked at population changes and voting patterns within North Carolina's one hundred counties. To do so, I analyzed the North Carolina Board of Elections' data on the total number of registered voters and identified the counties with the largest net increases of registered voters between 2008 and 2012. My purpose was to identify where voters were moving and see if those counties had changed their voting patterns between the two elections. If changes in a county's population of registered voters correlated with the county's shift in political support, I conjectured that demographic changes were stimulating shifts in North Carolina's elections.

To test this hypothesis, I analyzed all the counties with increases of 7,000 or more registered voters between 2008 and 2012. Of these eighteen counties, seven voted Democrat and eleven voted Republican in 2008.[xxvi] Despite a wide range geography and demography, each of these counties voted the same way in 2012 as in 2008. The addition of new voters into the counties did not alter how the counties voted. In fact, only five of North Carolina's counties changed how they voted between the two elections. Romney lost one county that McCain had won and captured four that McCain had lost. These four small counties, however, had a combined Republican vote of only 28,722 in 2012.[xxvii] From this data, I can conclude that demographic shifts of Democrats and Republicans do not explain Romney's victory in 2012. After reaching this dead-end, I turned my focus to voter turnout, hoping to discover whether this affected Obama's surprising win in 2008 and subsequent loss in 2012.

For this stage of research, I speculated that an abnormally high turnout in 2008 or an abnormally low turnout in 2012 could have given the victorious candidate the slight edge needed to win. In 2008, 61.6% of America's voting-eligible population[xxviii] voted for the president, while 65.5% in North Carolina did. The same pattern followed in 2012. While only 58.17% of the voting-eligible population cast their vote for president nationwide, 64.6% of North Carolinian voting-eligible citizens did.[xxix] This is abnormal for Southern states, both historically and recently. Politics in the Old South was characterized by low turnout rates, and Southern states have continued to produce lower turnout rates than the national average.[xxx] In 2008, only Virginia and Florida had turnout rates higher than North Carolina. These were the only three Southern states that voted Democratic. In 2012, only Virginia's turnout rate superseded North Carolina's, yet Virginia and Florida continued to vote Democrat while North Carolina reverted to voting Republican.[xxxi] This data, while inconclusive, shows a correlation between higher turnout rates and Democratic support in Southern states. However, this does not explain how Obama won in 2008 and lost in 2012 because it fails to illuminate *why* voter turnout rates were higher. I speculate that the high 65.5% turnout rate in 2008 contributed to the anomaly of Obama's win but cannot explain it alone.

After exploring voter registration, county in-migration, and voter turnout as possible explanations, I was unable to develop a conclusive theory as to why Obama won Colorado in 2008 and 2012 but won North Carolina only in 2008. Instead, I came to the conclusion that North Carolina is a state in transition. Obama's win in 2008 represents an irregularity in the state's voting trajectory instead of the beginning of a trend. J. David Woodard supports this idea in his discussion of North Carolina in *The New Southern Politics*. Woodard does not describe North Carolina as a "national state" but instead as an "emergent state." This categorization could help describe why North Carolina did not vote Democrat in 2012 like the national states of Virginia and Florida did. Woodard states that North Carolina is not a national state because, compared to other states, its rate of change is slow. While North Carolina is a national leader in research, finance, and education, it also fiercely defends its Southern roots and has large racial and economic divides. North Carolina is in transition, and the state holds both traditional and progressive ideals at the same time.

Woodard develops this idea when he writes, "The paradox of North Carolina is that it is stocked with tradition-minded citizens who are interested in newer ideas."[xxxii] If we applied this quote to the electorate in 2008, it could describe why Obama won North Carolina. North Carolinians may be tradition-minded, but they voted for the "newer idea": a young, charismatic, African-American candidate who inspired millions of Americans to hope for change. Obama also mobilized young voters who identify with the progressive side of North Carolina's character. According to 2008 CNN exit polls, 13% of North Carolinians said it was their first time voting. Of those respondents, 68% cast their ballots for Obama.[xxxiii] In addition, Obama won 74% of voters ages 18-29,[xxxiv] indicating that he appealed to a younger generation of voters who may feel disconnected from North Carolina's traditional roots. Obama was the "new idea" of which Woodard writes.

In 2012, Obama's novelty had run its course and North Carolinians returned to their traditional voting habits. This does not mean, however, that North Carolina is dependably Republican. North Carolina is a swing state precisely because of the tension between conservative and progressive ideas. It hovers between these two ends of this spectrum, and an individual candidate—not his or her political party—becomes the catalyst for moving along that spectrum. In 2008, Obama was able to mobilize voters and tilt the scale towards the more liberal side of the state's electorate. Although the same was not true in 2012, future candidates should look to Obama's win as an example and deliberately tap into the progressive ideas that counter North Carolina's traditionalist attitudes. In the words of Woodard, "North Carolina has room and the opportunity to grow in the years ahead."[xxxv]

During this exploration, I encountered a piece of data that seemed to contradict the logic of the 2012 outcome, especially in light of Obama's success in Colorado. Between 2008 and 2012, the number of registered Hispanic voters in North Carolina rose from 68,053 to 114,711.[xxxvi] This is a large increase for a four-year span, especially because these figures represent registered voters and not the Latino population as a whole. However, many factors explain why an increase in Latino voters did not lead to a Democratic victory in the state's elections. First, although the number of Hispanics grew rapidly, they still represent a small proportion of the state's population. Hispanics were 4.7% of North Carolina's population in 2000 and 8.4% in 2010. That is a 120% increase in ten years.[xxxvii] However, 8.4% is still small considering that Latinos made up 16.1% of America's population in 2010. In addition, the Latino share of registered voters is even smaller. In North Carolina, 1.7% of registered voters were Latino in 2008, and only 2.9% were Latino in 2012.[xxxviii] The Hispanic population is not large enough or voting with enough force to have a substantial impact on elections.

A second facet of the Hispanic presence in North Carolina supports this last assertion. Although there are many Latinos in North Carolina, a large proportion are not citizens and therefore are unable to vote. To put this in context, I will compare the Latino population in the Denver/Boulder area to the Latino population in North Carolina's three urban centers: Charlotte, Raleigh/Durham, and Greensboro/High Point/Winston-Salem. Latinos in the Denver/Boulder area constitute 23% of the area's total population. A full 76% of them are citizens, and only 29% are foreign born.[xxxix] This data indicates that the large proportion of and voting-eligible status of Latinos would give them increased political influence. Strength comes in numbers.

Compare this to North Carolina's Latinos, who average 10% of the population in the state's three urban centers. Only 56% of these Latinos are citizens, and a full 51% are foreign-born (Brown)[xl]. This indicates that far fewer Hispanics are voting because they are in North Carolina to work, not as citizens of the state. The foreign-born statistic supports this hypothesis because many undocumented workers come to the state with the goal of finding work in agriculture or manufacturing. Analyzing the Latino population in North Carolina's counties offers an additional perspective. Of North Carolina's one hundred counties, Duplin County has the largest proportion of Latinos. Latinos comprised 20.6% of the county's population in 2010, an increase of 1,088% from 1990.[xli] To understand why so many Latinos live in Duplin County, I researched its major industries. The county's top three employers are all pork and poultry processing plants.[xlii] Together, these three companies employ a full 22% of Duplin County's labor force.[xliii] It is reasonable to assume that jobs in the meat processing industry are the driving force behind the county's large Hispanic presence. Duplin County exemplifies the type of Latino who, because of lack of citizenship or influence in society, would not necessarily help a Democratic candidate win in North Carolina.

Despite these demographic realities, Democrats should not despair that North Carolina's Latinos cannot help them win. In fact, if Democrats are able to mobilize Latino voters, they can re-capture the state in future elections. The difficult part is mobilization. Nationally, the Latino voter turnout rate is lower than that of other racial groups. In 2012, only 48% of Hispanic eligible voters cast ballots in the presidential election. This turnout rate was 16.1% lower than that among whites and 18.6% lower than that among blacks.[xliv] This represents enormous untapped potential for Democratic candidates and their supporters. Because there were over 23 million eligible Latino voters nationwide in 2012, an increase of just a few points in Latino voter turnout could have a substantial effect on voting outcomes.

There is an inherent danger if the Democratic Party neglects to mobilize Hispanics, particularly because the Hispanic population is increasing so rapidly. If North Carolina's Latino population continues to grow but Latino turnout rates continue to lag behind, it is possible that counties with large proportions of Latinos will begin acting like Black Belt counties of the Old South. Black Belt counties are those in which a majority of the citizens are black. V.O. Key concluded that the higher the proportion of blacks in a given county, the more characteristically Southern that county's politics was.[xlv] The minority white population felt threatened and exerted their political power, thus repressing the majority black population. A modern-day version of this phenomenon could occur if the Hispanic population grows while Hispanic voter turnout stagnates, because white voters may begin to feel threatened by the increasing Latino presence in their counties. Based on Key's analysis of the Black Belt phenomenon, I hypothesize that if this happens, white voters will become increasingly politically involved in an effort to combat growing Latino influence. If voting eligible Latinos are not mobilized, they may become victimized by this system of political repression. This presents both a warning to Latino voters and an opportunity for the Democratic Party, because mobilizing Hispanic voters will help both groups in the long run.

V.O. Key's analysis of Southern politics also provides a warning to the Democratic Party. From the end of Reconstruction until the middle of the twentieth century, the Democratic Party took the South for granted. Both parties assumed that the South would always vote Democrat, so the Democrats did not focus on pleasing the South and the Republicans did not even attempt to win it. Beginning in 1948, however, Southern states began defecting from the Democratic Party. This eventually led to the "great white switch," in which the Southern states switched from the Democratic Party to the Republican Party and became the latter group's stronghold.[xlvi] If Democrats are not careful, the same could happen with their base of Latino voters. Even though Romney won only 21% of the national Latino vote in 2012, that means that over three million Latinos still voted for the Republican candidate.[xlvii] In addition, George W. Bush won 44% of the Hispanic vote in 2004, indicating that the Republican Party is capable of capturing large numbers of Latino voters if they have the right candidates and effective messaging.[xlviii] Although Hispanics currently vote Democrat in large numbers, the Democratic Party must be wary of taking the Latino vote for granted; if they do, they risk losing widespread support just like the Democratic Party lost the South by assuming its loyalty.

In an attempt to understand why Obama won Colorado in 2008 and 2012 but won North Carolina only in 2008, I discovered a promising trend in Colorado and inconclusive results in North Carolina. Colorado is experiencing rapid growth in its Latino and urban populations, and this demographic shift has put Colorado on a trajectory of future Democratic success. The 2008 election marked a turning point after which the Democratic Party has had an advantage over the Republican Party in Colorado. Conversely, it appears that Obama's 2008 victory in North Carolina was an anomaly indicative of the state's tension between traditional and progressive ideas. North Carolina is a state in transition. For now, it seems that North Carolina will border on the Republican side of the political spectrum until another charismatic Democratic candidate becomes the "newer idea" and shifts the balance left. If the Democratic Party can mobilize Latinos and retain their support nationwide, it should be able to repeat its 2008 success in swing states like North Carolina and Colorado while avoiding the setbacks of 2012.

[i] Dave Leip's Atlas of U.S. Presidential Elections. "United States Presidential Election Results."
2012. Web. 29 Nov. 2013.

[ii] Ibid.

[iii] Ibid.

[iv] The terms "Hispanic" and "Latino" will be used interchangeably in this paper.

[v] Leip, Atlas.

[vi] Mark Hugo Lopez and Paul Taylor. "Latino Voters in the 2012 Election." *Pew Research*
Hispanic Trends Project. Pew Research Center, 07 Nov. 2012.

[vii] Calculated using figures from Dave Leip's Atlas and Lopez of *Pew Research Hispanic Trends Project*

[viii] Leip, Atlas.

[ix] CNN Exit Polls: Colorado 2004, 2008, 2012. CNN Politics. Cable News Network, 2005, 2008,
2012. Web. 07 Dec. 2013.

[x] CNN, *Colorado 2004, 2008, 2012*.

[xi] Ibid.

[xii] Calculated using figures from Dave Leip's Atlas and Lopez of *Pew Research Hispanic Trends Project*

[xiii] U.S. Census Bureau. Colorado QuickFacts.. Generated by Zoe Rae Rote using American FactFinder. Web. 03 Dec. 2013.

[xiv] Calculated using data from the U.S. Census Bureau

[xv] "2008 Voter Registration Statistics" and "2012 Voter Registration Statistics." Colorado Secretary of State. State of Colorado, 2012. Web. 05 Dec. 2013.

[xvi] Leip, Atlas.

[xvii] Colorado Secretary of State, 2008 Voter Registration Stats.

[xviii] Leip, Atlas.

[xix] Leip, Atlas.

[xx] Calculated using figures from the North Carolina Board of Elections

[xxi] "Voter Registration Statistics" Statistical Data Search 2007 and Later. North Carolina State Board of Elections. Last updated 30 Nov. 2013. Web. 05 Dec. 2013.

[xxii] Calculated using figures Dave Leip's Atlas and the North Carolina Board of Elections

[xxiii] Earl Black and Merle Black. The Rise of Southern Republicans. (Cambridge, Massachusetts:
The Belknap Press of Harvard University Press, 2002) 241.

[xxiv] Leip, Atlas.

xxv Black, *The Rise,* 241.

xxvi North Carolina State Board of Elections, *Voter Registration.*

xxvii Leip, Atlas.

xxviii Voting-eligible population (VEP) is calculated by subtracting the populations that are ineligible to vote (such as non-citizens, prisoners, those on probation or parole, and ineligible felons) from the total voting-age population. It also factors in overseas eligible voters. VEP gives a more precise estimate of voter turnout than voting-age population data, because the latter does not take ineligible voters into account ("Voter Turnout").

xxix "Voter Turnout." United States Elections Project. Research conducted by Dr. Michael

McDonald. George Mason University, 22 July 2013.

xxx Ibid.

xxxi Ibid.

xxxii J. David Woodard. *The New Southern Politics.* (Boulder, CO: Lynne Rienner Publishers, 2006.) 95.

xxxiii CNN, *Colorado 2004, 2008, 2012.*

xxxiv CNN, *Colorado 2004, 2008, 2012.*

xxxv Woodard, *The New Southern Politics,* 98.

xxxvi North Carolina State Board of Elections, *Voter Registration.*

xxxvii U.S. Census Bureau. Profile of General Demographic Characteristics: 2000 Colorado.

xxxviii Barreto, Matt. "New 2012 Voter Registration Numbers Highlight Potential of Latino Vote in 9 Key States." Latino Decisions. 13 Aug. 2012.

xxxix Brown, Anna, and Mark Hugo Lopez. "Mapping the Latino Population, By State, County and

City." Pew Research Hispanic Trends Project. Pew Research Center, 29 Aug. 2013. Web. 08 Dec. 2013.

xl Brown and Lopez, Mapping the Latino Population.

xli Steven Mann and Gabriela Zabala. Demographic Trends of Hispanics/Latinos in North Carolina. Graphic "Percent Hispanic or Latino Population by County, 2010" produced 14 October 2011. Governor's Office of Hispanic/Latino Affairs.

xlii "Major Employers." Duplin County. Duplin County, North Carolina.

xliii Calculated using figures from the U.S. Census Bureau's "American FactFinder" feature

xliv Gonzalez-Barrera, Ana, and Mark Hugo Lopez. "Inside the 2012 Latino Electorate." Pew

Research Hispanic Trends Project. Pew Research Center, 03 June 2013.

xlv Key, V. O. Jr. Southern Politics in State and Nation. (New York: Alfred A. Knopf, Inc, 1949.) 6.

[xlvi] Earl Black and Merle Black. The Vital South. (Cambridge, Massachusetts: The Belknap Press of Harvard University Press, 1992.) Ch. 6.

[xlvii] Calculated using data from Gonzalez-Barrera and Lopez of the *PEW Research Hispanic Trends Project*

[xlviii] Rove, Karl. "Rove: About that 'Permanent Democratic Majority.'" The Wall Street Journal. 30 Jan. 2013.

www.ingramcontent.com/pod-product-compliance
Lightning Source LLC
Chambersburg PA
CBHW030354290526
45785CB00004B/1751